FROM NO WORTH TO SELF-WORTH

A COLLABORATIVE BOOK BY:

SHAWN LAURIE
CANDICE BAKX-FRIESEN
CHRISTINE ROSE
JASON FLOYD
JEAN KRISLE
KENNETH BATOR
KRISTINA SERVIDIO
MICHAEL MERRITT
PAT ROQUE
TAMARA PATZER
TREASHA McMANES
SEAN DOUGLAS

<u>Dedication</u>

Why do you second guess yourself?

Why do you think you're not good enough, beautiful enough, loved enough, wanted, or needed?

Who told you this and made you believe it?

Truth is, you never know someone is carrying around with them. You never know what someone has been through. A collection of moments and events in someone's life has brought them on this journey where you see them now, but that is not their destination. Sometimes we see a person at their highest and best, and other times we see them at their lowest and worst.

What we say and how we act becomes another moment of a person's journey. We have the ability to lift someone up or to tear them down. Where we are on our own journey influences that decision to lift or tear down, which is why with this book, we will have the ability to lift up people from all ages, backgrounds, and places, no matter where they are on their journey.

We dedicate this book to those who have ever been made to feel less than, to feel inadequate, been bullied, or held back. Everyone has something amazing to offer and we hope you will find inspiration within these pages to become a shining star. You were made for something GREAT!

TABLE OF CONTENTS

Introduction

Studies suggest that low Self-Esteem can lead to a tendency toward drugs or alcohol consumption. It's known that there is a cause-and-effect relationship between low Self-Esteem and addiction. The question is, which came first, the chicken or the egg? It's hard to tell which is the cause and which is the effect. Is the addiction a result of low Self-Esteem, or is the low Self-Esteem a result of addiction?

In some cases, having low Self-Esteem may be one of the reasons a person begins to abuse drugs or alcohol in the first place. In other cases, maybe they started out with good Self-Esteem, but addiction and its consequences damaged their ability to love themselves.

Self-Worth becomes a common denominator in this situation. A parent may be outwardly successful and happy, but inside they are doubting themselves and blaming themselves for poor choices their child has made, some leading to addiction.

There is not a parent on Earth that cannot instantly recall an incident in the past where they lost their temper with their child over something inconsequential, a time when they weren't where they should have been to protect their child, a time when they didn't follow the promptings they were feeling, or a time when they were completely out of control and the repercussions hit directly on the mental health of their child.

These situations often happen when the child is young or during the early teenage years, but it can literally happen at any time. The stress and reality of life are often the catalyst for a parent's lack of attention and time. It doesn't mean they don't love their child; it means they are not equipped to deal with their own anxiety and the pressures of life, and they unintentionally transfer their emotions to their children, either through their absence, or their reactionary communications. As a result, the child becomes unsure, feels unsafe, and is starving for approval, support, connection, and security. When the parent cannot, or does not, provide these needs, a child's sense of Self-Worth dissipates quickly. Just like the parent, the child will put on a good show outwardly, but inside, they are crying, unsure, and doubting themselves. As they look outside the home for a place to belong, they are often drawn to groups of kids who are also suffering from abandonment, abuse, or neglect.

The Self-Worth of both parents and children takes a hit when they are young, when they are hurting, and battling Mental Health issues. Thus, begins the downward spiral for the entire family.

Self-Love, Self-Esteem, and Self-Worth play a critical role in the choices we make throughout our lives. Connection and acceptance by one group over another also directly affects our choices. All humans want to be loved, accepted, and connected. If drugs and alcohol, and those associated with these actions, appear to be the only way to meet those needs, for a damaged soul it can be difficult to resist joining the group.

In this crazy world we live in, filled with both heroes and villains, love and hate, daisies and cocaine, it's important to love ourselves enough that we are willing to do the work, to stand up for ourselves, to believe in ourselves, and to make good choices.

- One out of every five (20.2%) students report being bullied. *(National Center for Educational Statistics, 2019)*
- A higher percentage of male than of female students report being physically bullied (6% vs. 4%), whereas a higher percentage of female than of male students reported being the subjects of rumors (18% vs. 9%) and being excluded from activities on purpose (7% vs. 4%). *(National Center for Educational Statistics, 2019)*
- Of those students who reported being bullied, 13% were made fun of, called names, or insulted; 13% were the subject of rumors; 5% were pushed, shoved, tripped, or spit on; and 5% were excluded from activities on purpose. *(National Center for Educational Statistics, 2019)*
- Bullied students reported that bullying occurred in the following places: the hallway or stairwell at school (43%), inside the classroom (42%), in the cafeteria (27%), outside on school grounds (22%), online or by text (15%), in the bathroom or locker room (12%), and on the school bus (8%). *(National Center for Educational Statistics, 2019)*
- According to a recent study, the absolute number of suicide deaths increased by 6.7% from 762,000 to 817,000 annually between 1990 and 2016, while age-standardized suicide rates fell by a third. Worldwide, the rates in 2016 were about 16 deaths per 100,000 men and 7 deaths per 100,000 women:

> women also experienced a greater decrease compared with men over the study period. *(Global Burden of Disease Study)*
> Suicide was the tenth leading cause of death overall in the United States, claiming the lives of over 48,000 people. *(Centers for Disease Control and Prevention (CDC) WISQARS Leading Causes of Death Reports)*
> Suicide was the second leading cause of death among individuals between the ages of 10 and 34, and the fourth leading cause of death among individuals between the ages of 35 and 54. *(Centers for Disease Control and Prevention (CDC) WISQARS Leading Causes of Death Reports)*
> There were more than two and a half times as many suicides (48,344) in the United States as there were homicides (18,830). *(Centers for Disease Control and Prevention (CDC) WISQARS Leading Causes of Death Reports)*

If you have doubts, please look in the mirror every single day and remind yourself, "I am enough. I have value. I am loved, and I love me." If you are tempted to make the wrong choice, please call a friend, call your sponsor, call someone. Please make a better choice, not just for you, but for generations after you, too. They are watching your example.

Suicide Hotline: 1-800-273-TALK (8255)

STOP Bullying Now Hotline: 1-800-273-8255

National Domestic Violence Hotline: 1-800-779-SAFE

National Sexual Assault Hotline: 1-800-656-HOPE

National Human Trafficking Hotline: 1-888-373-7888

National General Mental Health Hotlines:
https://www.pleaselive.org/hotlines/

Stop Abuse Resource: https://www.stopitnow.org/

Military Helplines:
https://www.tricare.mil/CoveredServices/Mental/CrisisLines

SAMHSA: https://findtreatment.samhsa.gov/

*This is not an inclusive list but these hotlines and online resources are available for those suffering, and for those who are tired of watching a loved one suffer. PLEASE use this resource and know that you are NOT alone!

Introduction contributed by 10,000 Beds, Inc. (10000beds.org)

Shawn Laurie: *Mastering Your Self-Worth*

Self-Worth is the most important thing we all need to develop before we can take our lives to the next level. No matter how far you want to go, learning your own Self-Worth is something that will change your life forever and will help you grow into a much better person no matter what your goals are. Let us look at what the true definition of "Self-Worth" is and what it means. We define "Self-Worth:" as, having an awareness of knowing one's own value or worth as a person. Having an opinion of yourself, believing if you are an amazing person and deserve a great life, or believing you are a terrible person and deserve a terrible life. Self-Worth is all about how you feel about yourself. Knowing and believing how valuable you are is a huge advantage when it comes to our personal development.

Now that you understand what Self-Worth is, let me tell you about my experience with my own Self-Worth and how I have figured it out and how learning to have Self-Worth changed my life. For many years, I had no idea what my own worth was, what it looked like, or what it even meant. I had no idea how important believing in myself was or understanding how much Self-Worth I had, and the truth is for a long time my life was falling apart. I was not only destroying my own life, but I was destroying everything around me. My own self issues were destroying a lot of lives around me. That life went on for about 10 years before I decided to make changes.

My new life started when I decided to make changes to become a better man. I started to learn what Self-Worth was and I started changing my outlook, not just in my life, but everything around me. I learned how I could use my own struggles to help me become successful and become an influencer for those that are struggling with what I had been struggling with for so long.

My life began to change once I finally found my Self-Worth again. Just knowing how much value my life held, I knew I was made for greatness. My first decision was to get clean and sober. That was the moment when everything got better, for not just me, but my family and those around me. Once you learn to love yourself and believe in yourself, you become a happier person taking yourself to a whole new level, and you become more enjoyable to be around.

Your behavior, your actions, and your decisions will soon reflect off your own thoughts of how you feel about yourself. You need to learn exactly who you are as a person. You need to know why you are the way you are. You need to understand yourself, love yourself, and care for yourself. If you want to be successful in life, then you need to learn all this, and more. Why would anyone invest or believe in you if you do not first believe in yourself? One of the main reasons we are losing so many people to suicide is because they have no idea how much value they hold. Once you understand that your life matters, you can choose your path to greatness any way you desire. I hope that you will learn how to love yourself again, and much more from this chapter.

You hold the power when you know and believe you can achieve your dreams with or without any disabilities. It takes time to get there, especially if right now you might be struggling with PTSD, Depression, or you are just struggling with a lack of hope and purpose. You are struggling with loving yourself. You are tired of failing and just want to give up. Whatever your situation is at this moment, just remember that right now you are in a different mentality and that is ok. Once you accept your situation, you will begin to open to a brand new you understanding your Self-Worth again and continuing the path to a brand new "you" which leads to changing your mindset.

I always remind people that the fact you are struggling with Self-Worth, Depression, or any other kind of problem, is that you are going to have issues. It is common to fight with yourself about certain difficulties, whether it is a physical or a mental disability. It is hard to deal with. The truth is that no matter the situation you are in, if you decide to make positive changes and stick with it, something is going to change inside of you and it is going to change your life. Even when you make it out of this situation you are fighting with, you are going to still have struggles. Just because you have a good life or do not have any mental struggles anymore, you will still struggle in some way or another. It is called being human. What I have learned throughout my struggles is that even a man with mental or physical disabilities will find a way to live life again if they choose to push forward. Somebody with a brain disability or somebody that has mobility issues still has a choice to live.

Learning to live with your disability is a huge part of building your Self-Worth. You must understand that even though you are struggling with some type of disability, the disability does not define who you are as a person. You are not your disability, and your disability is not you! Knowing your Self-Worth is going to play a key role in that, because if you know how much value you have, you will not describe yourself with PTSD, Depression, Anxiety, or any other issues. It is ok to recognize that you have something going on but never allow it to define you.

I want to discuss another "self-word" and that is, Self-Care. I see so many people that had a tough life with bad choices, disabilities, or even childhood traumas, and they just do not take care of themselves anymore. Most of them start drinking or self-medicating just to deal with the pain from the trauma or the mentality they are struggling with. I've talk to so many of them and most do not even get help because they feel like nothing can help them. So, they do not even try.

The point is that so many people have made it past their struggles. They have turned their "mess into their message" and that is exactly what I have done. My mission now is to just be there for them and show them there is a way to get better, and show people that there is a light at the end of the tunnel. Millions of us feel, or have felt, like there is no way out of the storm, but once you realize the only way to find yourself again is to fight through it, you push through the storm and get to the other side! My story has been told thousands of times, and I use it to inspire others.

When I first started going down that dark hole, it all began back in Afghanistan. I was rounding up halfway through my second tour when I injured myself on a mission. I jumped off a MRAP during a dismount mission and I landed wrong tearing my ACL and a partial tear of my meniscus. Long story short, I got sent to FT. Gordon for surgery and ended up spending two years there being medically retired, because even though I was there for surgery, I was told I was no longer deployable because I was being diagnosed with PTSD with Psychosis and Major Depression, among many other mental health issues I was struggling with. With everything going on, I was now being told within six months that I had to accept that my Military career was over. That was the beginning of eight long years of hell. It took me eight years to finally reach out and get the help I needed. I never though in a million years I would be here today telling my story and becoming an expert in my own mindset.

Once I woke up and realized that I controlled my own destiny, my life started to change. I found purpose again, leading to finding my Self-Worth. What changed is that I no longer allowed my mental health to define me, and I started giving myself the self-care that was needed so that I could help others. Self-care is something you must do for you. You must keep building yourself up and know your worth. You must start believing in yourself again, because nobody out here in this world is going to believe in you if you do not believe in yourself first. We all know this is not a nice world and things are not always fair. Life is hard and nothing is given to us. So, if you want something in life, you must get it and earn it.

Live with no more excuses! I have used this in my first book Veteran Mindset 2.0, and it has been absolutely life changing. I have used these three questions and so I will share it here with you. Another way I learned to find my Self-Worth is to ask yourself these three questions:

> ➢ Who am I at my Core?
> ➢ What am I struggling with?
> ➢ What do I want in life?

Ask yourself these three questions. Answer them honestly because if you never understand who you are, what you are struggling with, and what you really want, then you will never get to the next phase of your life. Once you have answered those three questions, study them and reread them over and over. Remind yourself on bad days what you want and what it takes to achieve it. Use them as notes to remind yourself of how far you have come and how far you want to go.

There are many of ways to help cope with your unhealthy mindset. You can learn different exercises and methods to achieve greatness. This book is a guide to do just that, to get you to a level you have never been before. Reading and understanding other people's perspectives and learning how to master your own Self-Worth from those who have been through it and are now at the next level makes all the difference.

Do what needs to be done and read this book. Every chapter is unique and beneficial in its own way. If you take this book seriously, you will start living your best life. You can make positive changes just by understanding and focusing on what you are reading and all you will need to do is apply it to your life. Always keep the positive people around you. Negativity can change a weak mind instantly. There are toxic people everywhere and they do not want to see us succeed, which is why staying focused on your mission is so important. Never allow the negativity of others to distract you from your goals.

There will be times you will want to give up, so when that happens, reread this book, and go back over everything you read or go over the three questions and the answers that you wrote down. When surrounded by negativity, it is always best to focus on anything that is positive. Remember, the opinions of others do not affect your Self-Worth. You have come this far and now there is no going back. You now know what it takes to get yourself to the top of your game. No more excuses! This is going to be the most difficult challenge you have ever had to take on, because it is not just a physical challenge, it is a mental challenge, too. That is why once you get the results that you want, it will be the most rewarding moment. Remember, anything in life that is hard is usually worth it. If it was easy, then everyone could do it and there would be no problems in the world, but it is not that way. One of my favorite lessons I enjoy talking about is my experience with hard and easy situations. The truth is that if I needed to make something happen and it was easy and did not take much effort, it really was not that big of a deal, and it did not mean as much in the end.

However, everything I have ever done or wanted to do, it was a challenge, it was hard to do, and it always turned out to be something amazing. That is just the way it is. The best thing about completing a tough challenge is that it always builds up your Self-Worth. That is your goal, right? You want to learn to love yourself again? You want to know how much value you hold? The only way to do that is to do the things you feel are challenging. There is power in having and understanding your Self-Worth. People see the confidence in you, and they see you are a winner. Self-Worth does that. It builds up your Self-Esteem and your confidence. Some of the biggest and most successful Entrepreneurs in the world will tell you that it starts with you believing in yourself. If you do not believe it, then it will not happen.

When someone asks me what the word "Power" means to me, I always answer with, Self-Worth. No matter what it is that you want to do with your life, you must have Self-Worth. You must know your value. Do I sound like a broken record yet? Hold on, let me say it a few more times for you. If you look down on yourself and do not believe in yourself, why would anyone else believe in you? Honestly, think about it. Unless they are a positive influencer, and it is their job to see the greatness in you, how would the average Joe or boss see greatness in you if you do not even believe that you matter or possess zero confidence? I will tell you this for a fact; it is a strong scent, I can see it, I can almost smell the lack of confidence in a person when I first meet them. It is like an animal smelling your fear.

Here is a little example about what I mean. Think about it like job interviews. If you are the type of person that your job interview experiences have always ended up with you getting the job, well more than likely you have a strong Self-Worth scent about you. If you never get a call back and never get hired on, then that is why. The smell is all over the room and the lack of confidence is all over your face. So where do you go from here? First, remember this, there is nothing wrong with you. Like I said earlier, you are not alone. If that was the case, then there would be no use for this book. I would not be able to talk about my experiences with my own lack of Self-Worth and then finding it again. So, one more time, it is important for you to know that you are not broken.

Only you know your story and know why your Self-Worth is lacking. At the same time, only you can change that. I can help you by giving you motivation and trying to inspire you with coping skills and different techniques, but YOU must make it happen. You must be willing to put in the work. A couple of things that worked for me was recording my achievements. The reason is because it reminds you that you are awesome and that you are capable of winning. Always remind yourself of the success that you have had in whatever you had to do, like school, jobs, challenges, etc.

Look at how far you have come in your journey. Whatever you have been through, recovery from drugs and alcohol, or it could be from mental health issues like Depression or PTSD, always remind yourself that you have come a long way from where you were. Whatever you have done that was important, and was life changing, always record it and remind yourself of it. Place yourself with winners and get away from toxic people. If you are surrounded by people that make you feel bad or put you down, you will never grow. Toxic people are the worst kind of people, they thrive off your misery. You are better than that. Never settle for less. Never take what you can get. You deserve the world, so you need to live like you know it.

The power of having Self-Worth will do just that. It will allow you to grab any opportunities that come your way. Keep a winning attitude and look for the positivity in everything around you. Even in bad situations, focus on the good out of it and not the bad. The reason this is important is because it is like a chain. If you think about positivity, you will want positivity. If you want positivity, you will look like positivity. If you look like positivity, you will attract positivity. If you attract Positivity, your life will be full of positivity. If your life is full of positivity, you will become Positive. If you become positive, you will feel more positive about yourself which means that you will begin loving yourself and BOOM! You understand your Self-Worth!

You see what I did there? The power of Self-Worth is more than you will ever know until you live that life. There are so many reasons that we do not feel great about ourselves, and I could author a whole book on Self-Worth being that it was one of my biggest struggles for so long, but for now, I will give you as much info as I can. With that said, if you are one of the millions of people that struggle with a lack of Self-Worth, just remember that you matter, and your life is important! You have the right to be happy and to be forgiven from anything that you have done in your past that you are not proud of. Start today, start right now, and start making the changes needed in your life.

Be proud of your accomplishments every time you reach a new goal. Write it down and when you feel like you are not moving forward, go back and read all the things that you have done. Set up new daily and weekly goals. This practice allows you to work toward something new in your life. Every time you achieve those goals, document it on paper or log it in your files somewhere you can gain access to it at any time. Remember, we cannot always rely on others to make us feel confident, successful, or important. We must do it for ourselves.

The last thing I want to say about Self-Worth is, accepting rejections. Many times, we feel low when someone or a company rejects us. We cannot always please everyone and there will always be haters. Let's talk about social media for a minute. I personally have about 68K followers at the time of writing this and well over 75 percent of them are supportive. However, there are still a few that no matter what I do, I will never be able to please them. Also, with those number of followers, you will have haters, those that want to put you down or make you feel bad about yourself. That is why loving yourself, and knowing your Self-Worth, is so important. The power of your Self-Worth allows you to shut down the negativity.

Once I learned my value, I no longer allowed anyone to hurt me or make me feel like I am not worth it. I made many bad choices for many years, but I have forgiven myself and have moved on to making momentous changes, not only in my life, but I have helped change thousands of others lives. You are an amazing person and unique in your own way. Stand up tall and build confidence in yourself. Begin living the life that you deserve. Remember the "Power of Self-Worth" will change everything for you if apply what you have learned in this chapter.

Good luck to you in your future and I hope that you make the changes you are looking for. I am proud of you for getting this far!

<u>BIO</u>

Shawn Laurie, A.K.A. the Veteran Guy, is a U.S. Army Combat Veteran completing two Afghanistan tours, 2007-2008 and 2010-2011. Shawn was injured in Afghanistan on his second tour and sent to Fort Gordon, GA, where he spent two years with the Wounded Transition Unit for ACL Reconstructive Surgery. Shawn was diagnosed with PTSD, major Depression, and severe Anxiety. He was finally retired from the Army in Oct 2012. Shawn has also struggled with opiate and Benzodiazepine addiction for 9 years. After many years of battling with his own demons and suicidal thoughts, Shawn lost his best friend from Ft. Gordon to suicide in 2016 and decided to make necessary life changes. He checked himself into a detox center and graduated six months later from an intensive outpatient rehab center. Shawn is the Founder of the Outreach Support Group Non-Profit Organization, VetLife4Life, and Authored his first book, Veteran Mindset 2.0. He's known as an Advocate, Ethos Speaker, Mindset Influencer & Consultant.

Website: https://www.vetlife4life.com

Facebook @ RealTalkWithShawn

Instagram @ RealTalkWithShawn

2

Candice Bakx-Friesen: *The Female Entrepreneur Mindset*

Few people understand the challenge of maintaining a sense of Self-Worth better than the Female Entrepreneur. About three-quarters of men and women start businesses to pursue an opportunity, rather than out of necessity, but men tend to be more confident of their eventual success. Even with similar levels of education and experience, men and women have drastically different views of their abilities. Why is that? Some may argue that women are hard-wired to be doubtful of their capabilities, but nothing could be further from the truth. The fact is, women have been exposed to far more boundaries imposed upon them by society and have to fight harder for the same opportunities, often for the most basic human rights. As you might expect, the impact this has on a woman's mindset and sense of Self-Worth is less than favorable.

The good news is that your mindset isn't set in stone. Even if you've held on to limiting thoughts and beliefs for years, you can create a new and empowering mindset that will lead you to success in both life and business. Let's look at a few key components of maintaining your sense of self-worth and entrepreneurial mindset.

Remember Why You Started

If you're a Female Entrepreneur, then you're well-acquainted with hard work, taking initiative, and seizing opportunities. While those things are important, the foundation of a winning mindset is knowing why you started in the first place. When you have complete clarity on your "Why," nothing will diminish your feeling of worthiness or deter you from achieving your dreams.

Have you ever faced a significant crisis in your life when you had to tap reserves of energy, grit, and courage, that you didn't even know you had? In those moments, your focus was laser-like. Your goal was compelling. Your mission was clear. If you've experienced this, then you've experienced the power of purpose. The purpose that drove you to do what you needed to do, when you needed to do it, is what is meant by knowing your "Why."

When times get tough, you need a mindset with an unshakable foundation. Whatever you wish to accomplish, in life or business, you're going to need clarity on **WHY** you're doing what you're doing. What drives you and keeps you motivated? What gets you out of bed in the morning and keeps you going even when things get hard? When you have pinpointed exactly what that is, you'll be unstoppable!

I've had a strong "Why" since I was a teenager. My grandparents came to Canada as refugees after World War II and losing everything. They worked hard to ensure that my mother, and their grandkids, had a good life. Their drive and dedication impacted my life in a big way, and I knew that I was going to carry that torch forward into my adult life. I do it to honor them, and to give the same degree of commitment to my own family. Never forget why you started, and remain humble by remembering where you came from.

Entrepreneurs often get hung up on *how* they're going to do something, rather than the reason *why* they're doing it in the first place. What purpose do you ultimately want to achieve? What changes in your life are you working to bring about? The answers to these questions will be your roadmap through the unknown and the fuel that keeps you going long after the emotion of motivation has faded. Remember the words of German philosopher Frederick Nietzsche: *"He who has a why can endure any how."*

Defeat Fear Through Action

It's common knowledge that confidence is a huge asset when it comes to achieving a goal, but what can you do when your confidence is lacking? Everyone knows fear kills opportunities, morale, and even relationships. Fear is formed when your mind becomes focused on the uncertainty of future outcomes. In other words, your mind freaks out about things that haven't happened yet, and may not even happen at all. What can you do when fear raises its ugly head and threatens to shut you down? You can stop and think about it, but thinking alone rarely conjures up confidence.

A common misconception is that every Entrepreneur is overflowing with self-control and confidence, which is simply not true. Entrepreneurs are always facing new challenges. Markets change, employees change, business growth leads to new challenges, and so on. Two constants faced by every Entrepreneur are challenges and changes, so get used to fear trying to creep into your mindset.

Every Entrepreneur, Leader, or Executive, is afraid of something. Yet, they succeed anyway. How? By taking action. Fear cannot exist in the same space as action, and while confidence helps, it's not a prerequisite for taking action. This truth is backed up by Neuroscience. The human brain can only consciously focus on one thing at a time. Once you are in the act of doing, your fear fades away. Therefore, taking action reduces conscious fear. This is the secret behind the success of many Entrepreneurs. When you feel fear, take action and watch the confidence follow.

Businessman and philanthropist W. Clement Stone described it well when he said, *"Thinking will not overcome fear, but action will."*

Choose Your Thoughts

Time spent alone with your thoughts can be positive, as well as an important part of your self-development and personal growth. The problem is that our minds are not always a safe haven. We all have an inner voice that can either direct us toward a healthy attitude about ourselves and circumstances, or toward a negative, more destructive outlook. Life is filled with situations that change and evolve, most of which you cannot control, but your world of thought is one area over which you have direct influence. One way in which many people get off track is allowing external circumstances to influence their thinking.

One of the most powerful mindset shifts is realizing that you have the power to choose your thoughts. No person or situation can dictate to you how to feel, only your thoughts can do that. Like everything in life that's worthwhile, it takes practice and effort to take conscious control of your thinking, but when you do, it's a game-changer! A great tip to help you with this is going back to your "Why." You'll be amazed at how your thoughts will shift and fall back into alignment with your goals when you remember the reason that's driving you.

Other People's Doubts Do Not Apply

Any time you set out to accomplish a goal or realize a dream, there'll be naysayers who vocalize their disbelief. Most people won't do it to be mean, but rather out of their own fear. Pursuing your dream involves a degree of risk, and when others see that you're willing to take a chance on yourself, it makes them uncomfortable. Oftentimes, those same people are unhappy in their own lives but are too fearful to make a change. They will often express their fears through doubt. They may doubt your resolve, capabilities, or willingness to see it through. This can be tough to endure, especially if it's coming from people that you respect and care about. Remember, you don't have to accept the limitations of others, nor do you have to adopt their fear-based views. Stay true to your vision and the belief that it's not only possible, but probable. You already believe your dream is possible or you would've never started in the first place. Remain steadfast. You're on a mission and you're equipped with everything you need to succeed.

Another thing I've found to be a huge benefit is surrounding myself with other Entrepreneurs who believe in collaboration and mutual support. If you don't have people like that in your life right now, I highly recommend hiring a Coach. You need to have someone in your corner who will give you the support you need.

Realistic & Flexible Expectations

What does it mean to have realistic expectations? Does it mean that you only set goals that are easy to achieve? Not at all. It simply means that what you desire to achieve can be accomplished in a sensible amount of time. Expectations directly impact your attitude and mindset. If you exceed your expectations, you tend to have a positive attitude and mindset. If you don't meet or exceed your expectations, you tend to have a less-than-stellar attitude and mindset. By creating realistic timeframes for your goals, you'll perpetuate your positive mindset as you move from one victory to the next.

One of the first things every Entrepreneur learns is that even the best laid plans can go awry. You can prevent a lot of frustration by learning to be flexible. There are too many variables to guarantee that everything will always go according to plan. In fact, that's usually the exception. This doesn't mean that you change your goals; it just means you're flexible on how you go about achieving them.

While we're on the subject of expectations, let's talk about the comparison trap. It's easy to begin comparing your life (or business) to others and feel like you're falling short, especially if it seems like everyone else has their act together and they're enjoying one success after another.

I'll never forget the time a friend shared with me that he was about to enter his third year in business, and was finally going to turn a profit. I was shocked! On social media he appeared to be successful and very well connected, yet it took three years of perseverance for him to be profitable.

People often shy away from sharing their struggles, and I admired my friend even more for sharing his with me. It underscored for me the importance of never comparing your situation to someone else's.

Remember, things are seldom what they seem on the surface and the Entrepreneurs you look up to face many of the same challenges you do. They may not advertise their challenges on social media, but they have them I assure you.

Protect Your Mindset Through Boundaries

In a world that considers hustling 24/7 a badge of honor, it would be easy to assume that you have to be "on" every minute of every day. Despite many so-called gurus who advise others of the need to work around the clock in order to succeed, the reality is that it can lead to exhaustion, poor health, and burn out. Determine when and where to place your focus, and stick to it without apology. The idea is to design your business around your life, not the other way around. There'll be times when you may have to burn the candle at both ends, but it doesn't have to be your lifestyle. Protect your personal and family time (and your sanity) by creating boundaries. They will help you stay energized, on task, happy, and healthy.

Your time and energy are valuable assets, and there's a finite amount of both. How you leverage those assets will impact your personal growth and well-being, as well as, the difference that you make in the world. Boundaries aren't the same for everyone, and they can change over time, so check in with yourself from time to time and see where you stand. How far are you willing to go to succeed? What are you willing to sacrifice, if necessary? How much time are you willing to devote? By understanding your boundaries, you can apply consistent effort and avoid burnout.

There may be times when, as you grow and become more successful as an Entrepreneur, you notice when some friends change or begin treating you differently. It can be frustrating, and you may miss the relationship you once had with them, but remember that your boundaries are important, too. Sometimes, you must change people, places, and other things in your life in order to continue your personal growth and success in your business.

Value Your Time

As previously mentioned, your time is a finite resource. You can make more money, build new relationships, or find new resources, but you can't put more hours in a day. Valuing your time can mean different things to different people, and you'll have to decide what it means for you. Perhaps it means charging more for your time, or maybe it means working less. The bottom line is that you're defining what your ideal life looks like, and no one can decide that but you. If you allow other people to define it, you're not valuing your time as much as someone else's opinion. That will typically lead to feelings of resentment and unhappiness.

Another way to value your time is by delegating certain tasks to others. If you started a business out of love and passion, then there are likely things that you adore doing, and things you dislike doing. The key here is to maximize the time that you spend doing the things that you love, and minimizing the time spent on things you do not. Delegating is one way to do that.

Let's talk about money. How much money do you need to live the life you want to live? Don't skimp here, and remember to factor in all expenses. Once you have that number, you can create a plan to generate that income. Doing this will help you further target how you spend your time. Ultimately, valuing your time is how you design the life you want to live.

Your Business Doesn't Determine Your Self-Worth

The pressure to succeed can be overwhelming. This is especially true for Female Entrepreneurs who often feel as though they must prove themselves. The good news is that you have nothing to prove to anyone but yourself. You chose the entrepreneurial path because you know you have what it takes to succeed. That said, understand that your Self-Worth isn't based upon the behavior of your business. Every business venture has its ups and downs. There are times when everything seems to go right and you're on top of the world, but then there are times where nothing seems to work and the business struggles to survive. This is normal and every entrepreneur has had such experiences at one time or another. None of that is a reflection of your worth.

We live in a world where many people judge their worth, and the worth of others, by material success. Basing your worth on the success of your business is a slippery slope, because there are simply too many factors outside of your control that directly impacts your business. As a Certified Money Coach, I frequently work with people who have tied their sense of Self-Worth to the success of their business. I've seen too many Entrepreneurs fall for the lie that their Self-Worth is tied to their net worth, and it's my mission to help break those negative beliefs about money.

Remember, your Self-Worth is based upon who you are, not your business or anything outside of yourself. When you know who you are, and are happy with the person you've become, you'll experience a sense of peace that will carry you through life's ups and downs.

Defy Societal Expectations

As a Female Entrepreneur, you're already defying many societal expectations placed on women. It's beyond the scope of this work to delve into the reasons why so many societies hold the belief that women are inferior to men, even if subconsciously, but we have to acknowledge that such beliefs exist. Historically, women were supposed to choose feminine jobs and men were supposed to lead. This viewpoint evolved over hundreds of years based upon the role of men and women in the survival of the species. These days, with the advent of industrial and medical revolutions, many of the old techniques necessary for survival are no longer necessary.

The world of business still tends to be male-dominated, but this has been slowly evolving over the last few decades. You, as a Female Entrepreneur, are part of this change. Understanding your role in this is vital to your mindset and sense of Self-Worth. You're not only working for your own success, but for every woman who will follow in your footsteps.

The best advice I can share with you is to remain true to yourself. You don't have to adopt the attitudes or behaviors of men in order to be successful. As a woman, you bring to the table your own set of skills and advantages that will help you as a leader and a businesswoman. Being self-aware is the key, and also accepting the fact that you're every bit as capable as a man. You're allowed to own your accomplishments just as much as you're expected to accept your mistakes. Continue to dream the big dreams, celebrate your victories, and boldly walk into your future.

Ask For Help

A common trait among many Female Entrepreneurs is the feeling that it's not okay to ask for help. After all, if you believe you have to prove yourself because you're a woman, it's a short jump to the mistaken belief that you need to do everything on your own. The reality is that no one, male or female, does it all alone.

Understanding your need for a strong support network, in order to succeed as an Entrepreneur, is crucial to a heathy mindset. The familiar adage, "It's not what you know, it's who you know," holds true in this case. You need to have people in your circle you can count on when you need them. Let go of the idea that you have to manage everything alone, and lean on others when needed. No one expects it of you, and it wouldn't matter if they did.

Be intentional when building your team. Naturally, you want to be surrounded by people with whom you have a good rapport, but you also want those who will positively challenge you. You have your own set of strengths, but you also have areas in which you need support. Look for individuals who can help fill the voids. Whether it's computer skills, creativity, communication, or anything else, you need people who bring different strengths and skills to the table. If those individuals are also highly adaptable and can roll with life's inevitable changes, you'll have a team that is nearly unstoppable! Delegating tasks, letting go of micromanaging, and asking for help could be a learning curve, and may require a shift in your mindset, but the effort is worth it.

There are many ways for you to find entrepreneurial success. It takes hard work and persistence, but most of all it takes a winning mindset.

<u>BIO</u>

Candice is passionate about helping people reach their financial dreams. She is a highly motivated woman who has a passion for helping others succeed in life and business. She is a mother of 4, top performing realtor, entrepreneur, money coach, and speaker. Candice has been a real estate investor since 2001. Candice's candid approach to business and affinity for getting past the fluff and getting to the root of each challenge for her clients so that they get a lot done, has led to her becoming a highly sought-after coach within the finance and real estate industries. She also provides sales coaching to fellow real estate agents but her passion lies in the finance industry. She coaches / trains / mentors on money topics, anything from basic budgeting to real estate investing. Candice has had many opportunities to speak in front of large crowds and enjoys teaching others and helping people reach their financial dreams.

https://www.candicebakxfriesen.com

https://www.facebook.com/InvestorSmarts

https://podcasts.apple.com/ca/podcast/investor-smarts/id1443677340?mt=2

Treasha McManes-Weimer:
A Measure Of Purpose

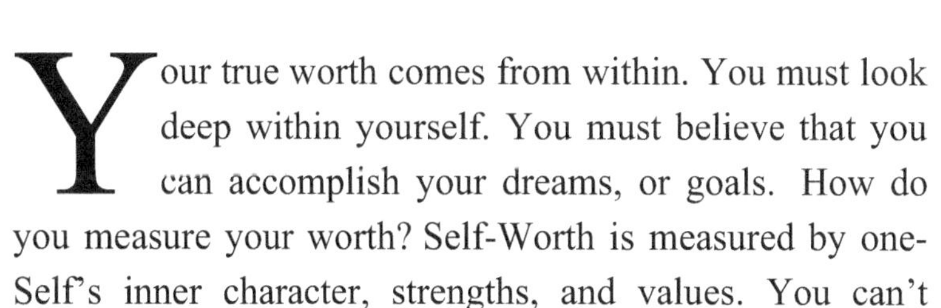

Your true worth comes from within. You must look deep within yourself. You must believe that you can accomplish your dreams, or goals. How do you measure your worth? Self-Worth is measured by one-Self's inner character, strengths, and values. You can't determine or measure your worth by the amount of financial success, number of friends, or having a nice big house.

Sure, it is great to have all those things, but does it make you happy? It is measured by how you see "Your-

Self." That doesn't mean to be cocky, but it means to be proud of who you are. To find your inner character is to define your struggles or weaknesses.

Be comfortable and confident with who you are. Go with what your gut is telling you. Keep reminding your-Self that you are worth it. There is no limit, you deserve the best. Be your own superhero in your life. Take those negative characteristics, turn, and embrace that negativity into a positive solution.

Some people in life lose their self-confidence, normally through any type of trauma. They fear that others will judge them based on appearance, their past, or just can't take criticism well. This leads them to verbally put themselves down, or isolate themselves to prevent any more damage, constantly reminding themselves that they will not and cannot succeed. They think they are failures and will never mount to anything. They feel worthless. I call this the "inner critical coach." This is where comparing your-self to others is common with those who have low Self-Esteem. Sometimes it's easy to just shut down and walk away, right? Hide from problems because it's too painful or too hard? I'm here to explain that is not the right answer.

I, too, thought this way growing up. All my life I struggled to find my-Self. I grew up in a Military home. I was taught to be a perfectionist. Everything had to be perfect and in a certain way. I was afraid to make mistakes. I knew if I made any mistakes, I would be punished, or even criticized. This made me afraid to make any decision independently. So, I always wanted to seek positive feedback or approval before I made any decisions. I worried about what people would say, do, or think about me. As a Military kid, I was constantly moving to different places and going to different schools, so it was hard for me to find friends. I wanted so badly to fit in. I was made fun of because I was the new kid. I was bullied in middle school. I would talk differently or look weird. I was tired of the bullying and harassment. I wanted to change my appearance. I wanted to be like everyone else.

At 15 years old, I began to rebel against any adult authority. I would steal from others just to get what I wanted. I hung out with gangs, drank, and did drugs every night. I dropped out of school at 16 years old. I was running the streets and sold my body just so I can have money to pay for my fix. I became aggressive and verbally abusive. I fought anyone who looked at me wrong or said something wrong. I was always in trouble with the law. I didn't care about anyone I hurt, including my-Self. I was on a path of self-destruction. I tried several times to commit suicide by cutting my wrist. It wasn't until a juvenile officer informed me that my life was worth more. She inspired me to become greater. She told me to embrace my past failures. I didn't understand what she meant until I became a parent.

I wanted to make a better life for me and my two children. In 2006, I was in a toxic relationship. Every night, I was put down and talked down to by my boyfriend. He would drink every night. He verbally, emotionally, and mentally abused me. To him, I was simply worthless, and a failure. He never supported me on anything that I was proud of or had a passion for. Everything had to be his way. I was tired of being treated like I was nothing. I went back to school and passed my GED. I was so excited and so proud of myself. I was starting to gain confidence. I knew that I had to leave that toxic relationship, not only for me, but for my kids, too. I wanted to make sure they were safe.

I was so excited about getting my GED, I wanted to continue my education. I then went to a community college. In 2012, I graduated with an Associate's Degree in General Arts. I then remember how I was inspired by the female juvenile officer. I decided that I wanted to help at-risk youth. I wanted to make a difference and inspire young people so that they can change.

I became a Juvenile Supervision Officer in 2012. In 2014, I was even more motivated to go back to school and I graduated in 2017 with a Bachelor's Degree in Criminal Justice. A month later, I was promoted to Juvenile Probation Officer.

I started to gain more confidence and more passion in my-Self, until I had become overwhelmed with emotions. Every day I was stressing my-Self out. I was second guessing a lot of my decisions, to the point that I was suspended without pay because I missed an important document. I wanted to be the best Probation Officer and the fear of failing at my job scared me. One day, I got the news that we lost a juvenile to gun fire. He shot himself in the head at 14 years old. Two weeks earlier, he was locked up in our facility. It hit me hard. I felt like a failure. I felt like I let this kid down.

After my passion faded, I started to turn to God. I started to read the Bible every night before I went to bed. A Bible verse would come to mind when I started to have negative doubts about my-Self and who I was. *"She is clothed with dignity and strength and laughs without fear of the future."* Proverbs 31:25. This verse has a meaning that struck me. She is clothed means my spiritual well-being. Dignity & strength was my strong-willed go get it attitude. There I knew what my purpose, and my true worth was. I was to keep pushing forward. I got rid of my negative thoughts. I started to believe in my-Self once again. I started to believe that I was greater than what I was telling my-Self.

One day, I saw juveniles out in town. Each one came up to me and told me their lives had changed for the better. They thanked me with hugs. They would say, "Because of you caring, you changed my life." Nothing gave me more joy and honor than when they said those words to me. It was like a heavy weight was lifted off my shoulder. I knew I couldn't save them all, but I then understood that if I can change one life, I made a difference in many.

To find my Self-Worth was important. I knew I had to make a change. To know who I truly was has inspired and motivated me to become the person that I am today. It did not happen overnight, of course. To find my worth took many years. I had to search inside my-Self to find my worth and my purpose. Sure, I had a rough path. I had self-doubt, low Self-Esteem, and no confidence in my-Self. I kept pushing and digging deep within my-Self to find my purpose. I thought that I would never find my way. My negative attitude was letting me down. I had to find my-Self. I found that I had to start caring for my-Self. I always had a passion for music and always wanted to learn to play guitar, so I began teaching myself how to play. Another way that I took care of my-Self was to take a long hot bath, or even go for a walk. It may sound a bit selfish to take time for your-Self, especially, when you are taking care of your-Self, but it is not. It is completely ok. Sometimes, you need to put you first in order to find who you are.

You are important. You are your superhero, and you choose your destiny. Don't ever let anyone stop you, not even your-Self. Kick out your inner critic coach and listen to your heart. I learned to stop listening to negative people, or believing what was on social media. Block all negative things or toxic people. Be happy, blessed, and grateful for what you have accomplished. Find positive people, or positive hobbies, that will make you happy. It is time to focus on you!

That is what I did and kept moving forward. Yes, I was a survivor of a toxic lifestyle. I was able to leave that lifestyle for the better by letting go of all toxic negative people. Those negative people were only bringing me down. For years I was not happy. I was not going anywhere but down a path that led me to destruction. My mess gave me my passion. My passion gave me my future. I am a Mother, a Wife, a Sister, & a Daughter who loves her family. I am a great Probation Officer because I made a difference in youth's lives. I had to fail in life in order to succeed. I found out that I don't need to be perfect because no one is ever perfect. I'm successful because of my own story and what I have become through my mess. I never regret my past struggles, but instead, choose to embrace my past struggles. That is why I am who I am today. This is who my-Self is. This is my measure of purpose.

<u>BIO</u>

Treasha McManes-Weimer has a Bachelor's Degree in Criminal Justice Administration and her field of work is Juvenile Justice. She has two certifications in Juvenile Supervision Officer (JSO), and Juvenile Probation (JPO). Treasha currently works at the Juvenile Justice Center in Abilene, Texas, as a Certified Juvenile Probation Officer in the Intake Unit, but also works at JSO Corrections. Her passion and goal are to change the lives of at-risk youth and helping them to become successful in our community.

TikTok - @trehouse_po
Facebook - @Tre McManes

Kenneth Bator: *My Formula Applies To Me, Too*

It's 6 AM on Monday, February 24, 2020, and I'm heading to the airport to go home from a trip two days earlier than expected. I am dead tired having had two hours of sleep at best, but my mind is racing. That's what hitting rock bottom will do to you.

I had thought I had hit rock bottom before in my life, but I was wrong. When I got fired in 2001 from an executive position that I had worked so hard to get, and was so proud to have reached that level by the age of 30, it was a big blow to my Self-Worth. That time in my life was bad, but not like this.

When the Great Recession hit and I had to take significant losses on not one, but two events my business rolled out in 2009 and 2010, that was bad, but not like this. That's a big blow to your Self-Worth, as well as your wallet, when your ego overrides your logic.

I bounced back after both of those periods in my life, but that was nothing like this. Absolutely nothing like that last weekend in February 2020. Little else completely and brutally beats you down to the ground and keeps pummeling you like alcoholism does.

On the surface I was the B+C+S guy. That was "The Formula for Business Success" I wrote about in my book in 2015. B+C+S stands for Brand, Culture, and Strategy. In other words, the formula answers three important questions:

➢ What is the image I want to promote to the public?
➢ What is the experience I need to create?
➢ How do I drive more of the right business to my business?

The image, or the "B," that I portrayed, or at least I thought I was portraying, was that of a succesful Entrepreneur that was also a "functional alcoholic." It even got to the point where I used that phrase to describe myself. I would be meeting a fellow professional during a business function and receive the ubiquitous question of, "So, what do you do?" My answer would be something like, "Other than being a functional alcoholic?" Stating it with a mixed drink or glass of wine in my hand, of course.

I think I made sure to stress the word "functional" as if I was trying to make myself believe it. Frankly, I'm not quite sure when I even adopted that title. Maybe it was in 2008 when I was walking on the shoulder of a freeway at 7AM trying to find my hotel after a very long night out, but I was still "functional."

Maybe it was in 2014 when I woke up in an alley after the last night of a business trip not having any idea how I got there, but I was still "functional."

Maybe it was in 2019 when I woke up on the bathroom floor of my hotel room with my nose broken and my white shirt completely soaked in blood, but I was still "functional."

Maybe it was all those mornings I needed to grab every receipt in my pocket to try to piece together what I did and how much financial damage I may have caused the night before, but I was still "functional."

That was the experience, or the "C," I was living. Although the brand I created, or the one I thought I did, was one of business success, the truth was, that everything earned was very quickly going to alcohol first, and then strippers, gambling, food, and probably a number of other things I will never fully remember.

There was nothing functional about the weekend that began on February 21, 2020. Over twenty years of hiding a problem I didn't even fully realize that I had, finally reached a critical point. It was a weekend that by its conclusion had become all too familiar with the combination I just mentioned, except for the gambling. There wasn't a casino anywhere near the place that I was staying, otherwise gambling may have been added to my list of activities those past couple of days. The result of that weekend was me preparing myself to basically lose everyone and everything that was important to me as I was on that Lyft ride to the airport the morning of February 24th. I had been hiding so much of the carnage from my alcoholism for so long that I felt I had to prepare for massive rejection. This was especially true in that the carnage was comprised of so much damage – physical, emotional, financial, and spiritual.

When I discuss the B+C+S Formula, I often use the analogy of an iceberg. It helps me to explain to an audience or a client that only a portion of the Brand, Culture, and Strategy is seen "above the waterline."

Now that my wife had learned more than just the tip of the iceberg, I had to explain the depths of how far that sucker reached under the water. I knew how painful that would be and thought that I better prepare to be kicked out of my home. If that happened, I had to come up with a backup plan. The next logical step would be to stay with my parents for a few days or weeks until I could figure out the next best move. I deduced that I had better call my father when I get off the plane to give him a heads up that he and my mother may be seeing me a lot sooner than my next planned visit. Doing so would mean that I would have to give him gory details as to why, and he didn't even know about the tip of the iceberg, much less know that a problem even existed! Simply put, we alcoholics are really good at hiding secrets. How disappointed would he be?! I know he didn't raise me to be what I had become. Would the disappointment cause him to hang up the phone and never take my call again? I certainly woudn't blame him if he did, I thought.

The strategic-planning facilitator in me, the "S" of my formula, knew that I had to have a third option as well. That could take on many different forms, but they would all be very short term in nature. I could stay at a hotel for a few days, or even weeks, to get my bearings and figure out a next step, but exactly what would that next step be? I could stay with friends for a night or two, but then I would have to share at least some of the details as to why. All of my friends are good people, though. They are upstanding citizens, parents, professionals, etc. In other words, these are people with Self-Worth. If they even got a glimpse of the piece of garbage that I had become, why would any of them even talk to me ever again, much less invite me into their homes?!

I drank to forget about my failures. I drank to forget about losing that executive job that I was so proud of earning two decades earlier. I drank to forget about the mistakes that I made as an Entrepreneur. For a few hours, that worked, but it always resulted in more problems the next day. Then I had to drink to forget about those complications. Then when I would realize how many problems I had caused and how big of a hole I had dug for myself, I drank to forget all that. When all of these combined issues led me to believe how little Self-Worth I had, I drank to forget that and feel better about myself, even if I knew it was just for a few hours until I passed out somewhere.

On this early Monday-morning ride to the airport, there was nothing to help me forget. There was nothing but a "no-worth" feeling as I sat with a tidal wave of thoughts crashing down on me…none of them good. Then the worst thought of them all came to me. What if everyone I knew rejected me when they find out what I have become? What if my wife left me? What if my parents disowned me? What if my friends never wanted to have anything to do with me ever again? What if I lost every client and business colleague once they realized that there was nothing to the brand I thought I created. Nothing "functional," but all "alcoholic." That was a distinct possibility. Then I would truly be alone.

As that thought rolled to the forefront of my consciousness, I felt something and heard, "But *I* will be here!" I know not everyone will share my beliefs and level of faith. Some will say that it was simply what my psyche manifested because it was what I needed at the time. Others may say that it was my "higher power" which is what I choose to believe. Either way, I felt a sense of peace that I had never felt before. My thoughts changed to, "I have to do this, and I can do this, whatever 'this' turns out to be."

The next few days and weeks were hard. Extremely hard. Some people were hurt. Some people were angry. Some were upset. Some were confused. I had laid all of my cards on the table and came clean with everyone with whom I needed to. I was humbled…more so than I had ever been in my entire life.

To my immense surprise, I did not find myself in isolation. No one left me. My wife, while upset, offered to find help for me. My father showed a level of compassion that I had not even experienced as a child. My friends each responded with some form of, "I'm here for you," or "Let me know if you need to talk." I even heard more than one,

"I'm proud of you" when sharing that I was attending daily AA meetings. This was a far cry from the thoughts that I had during that Lyft ride on February 24th.

One of the most important conversations that I had that day was with my neighbor and friend who has been sober for decades after his own bout with alcoholism. On my trip home that day, one definitive plan that I made was that I obviously and clearly needed help, and I was going to do what I needed to find it. I had decided before even getting off the plane at LAX that, regardless of whether or not I had alienated everyone I knew, alone or not, I was going to find assistance in what ever form that took. I was going to find some shred of Self-Worth again. That was the new "S" to begin building a new "B" and "C" for my personal formula.

After spilling my guts to my father and my wife, I walked to my neighbor's house later that afternoon. I asked him to tell me about Alcoholic Anonymous and what was involved. He shared the details and gave me a challenge without any judgement. I wholeheartedly accepted that challenge and we talked some more. As we ended that conversation, I thanked him and began to get up to leave. He could tell that I was obviously at my lowest point and he said something that I will remember for the rest of my life. He said, "Everything will eventually be OK. Some day you are going to be the guy sitting across from somone that is in the same situation that you are in today, and you are going to help him just like I'm helping you."

Over the course of the next few weeks, I received and felt more support than I had felt in decades as I was starting to build and regain some sort of semblance of Self-Worth again. I often tell my clients that we need to work on the core problem of their business and not just work on the symptoms, otherwise, we won't make any significant progress. After just a few days of being in AA, I felt that I had finally discovered my core problem; exactly what was holding me back, not only in business, but in life. I dove into my business, my marriage, my relationships, and so much more with a renewed energy.

In early March 2020, less than 30 days of being sober, I was able to attend a conference and its related evening activities, not only without drinking alcohol, but also without feeling like I was missing anything. Boy did that feel good! The evening of March 11, 2020, I'm hanging out at the hotel bar with my colleagues drinking a Sprite like it was natural, rather than what had become my usual vodka and club soda. I'm feeling really good when I look up at the TV screen to read, "The NBA has suspended all games and its season indefinitely due to the coranvirus." All of a sudden I felt like I was in a scene from the 1980 movie, *Airplane!* "I guess I picked the wrong time to quit drinking!"

That began an unprecedented time with a cascade of challenges no one could ever predict. Those challenges had me scrambling, like many Entrepreneurs and Executives around the world, to pick up the pieces and find a way to keep both of my businesses moving forward. If I couldn't move them forward, at least keep them on life support.

One of the things that I learned very early in AA is that alcoholism is a disease that thrives on self-pity. Through the stories I heard and the pages I read, I recognized a lot of similarities of my feeling-sorry-for-myself moments leading to my let's-drink-to-forget experiences.

By mid to late March, that self-pity didn't just creep back into my life, it walked though the door like an old friend yelling, "Hey, remember me old buddy?!" Soon that false friend had me complaining to my higher power, the one that gave me so much peace exactly when I needed it in that Lyft ride about a month previous. "You inflict me with this awful disease of alcoholism. I finally figure out the core problem that I have. I get the help that I need and start working on it with all my heart and mind. I start moving forward in a way that I hadn't done in decades and now you throw this coranavirus-pandemic crap at me! Why?!" I'm not sure if I said this out loud or just thought it but that was certainly what I was feeling practically word for word.

I didn't expect an answer but I got one. Again, whether you believe the response came from my higher power or my psyche is immaterial. The fact that I heard this loud and clear is relevant. "If you were not sober during this pandemic, you never would survive it. You would crawl into a bottle and never come out," the voice said.

I knew that answer to be true. Despite the self-pity, I knew that in the first week of the pandemic I had exemplified more leadership than I had in years, maybe decades. Leadership ran deep with the clients of Bator Training & Consulting at a time when they needed it. Leadership for the members of the Police Officers' Credit Union Association (POCUA) when they had to hear it. Leadership for my friends and colleagues because it was just the right thing to do.

While my proclivity to fall into a dark place had not dissipated, and quite possibly never will, I had developed the tools to avoid reaching for a bottle of Vodka. Did I still want to? Of course! But instead of thinking, "Let's get a drink so I can forget all this," the neural pathway led to, "If I drink to forget all this then I will for awhile but I will be left with bigger problems in the morning." What I had learned in a short time allowed me to perservere through the dark place and make a different choice…a better choice…a choice someone with Self-Worth would make.

I know full well what a pandemic "shelter-in-place" scenario would have looked like without sobriety. It would be frustration, anger, and despair by 1:30 PM and the twisting open of a Vodka bottle by 2 PM. It would be passing out shortly after dinner in the living room chair before 9 PM. It would be my wife gently shaking me awake at 9:30 PM suggesting I go to bed. It would be me waking up around 3 AM in bed wondering how and when I got there. It would be sleeping until 10 or 11 AM, having some coffee and aspirin, and trying to perform something that seemed like working. Then a repeat of what had happened the day before around 2 PM.

That's not what the pandemic looked like in reality for me because of my sobriety. Instead, I was finding a way to keep my clients for the right reasons and helping their business through this insanity while staying sane myself. It was finding ways to keep the POCUA afloat while also providing additional value to its members during this difficult time. Everyday at 7:30 AM I was at my desk ready to work and ready to figure this out, still with coffee but without the aspirin. Many times at 2 PM I was preparing for a 3 PM video meeting rather than looking in the freezer to see if I had a full bottle of Vodka. At 6 PM I was developing new ideas that I wanted to implement to move myself and my business forward. At 10 PM I was lying in bed holding my wife's hand and knowing that I would actually remember this entire day when I woke up the next morning.

It woud have been very easy to crawl back into a bottle. In March 2020, I had a better excuse than most of the other ones that led me to turn to alcohol to forget. I'm certainly not cured. I will be treating my alcoholism for the rest of my life, but I choose to perservere through the urge and into leadership because I feel the Self-Worth. Whether my decisions are good or not, I will not only remember them, but also have the capacity to make a lot more of them. With increased Self-Worth and clarity, I am confident that the majority of those decisions will be good ones and that I will truly learn from the ones that don't turn out the way that I had planned.

My new Self-Worth reminds me to tell myself, as I told many prospective clients in the past, my B+C+S Formula applies to you, too! It's still a work in progress, but I am building an image in the public eye that I am proud of. I am creating an experience that is healthy and supports what I want to accomplish. I am finally driving more of the right business to my business.

<u>BIO</u>

Ken is the Founder of Bator Training & Consulting, Inc. (BTC), as well as the Police Officers' Credit Union Association (POCUA), and has more than 20 years of experience in helping organizations reach new levels of effectiveness by aligning their brand, culture, and strategy. He is the Author of, *The Formula for Business Success = B + C + S,* and, *The Pocket Guide to Strategic Planning: The 90-Day Quick Fix for the Business Owner or Manager*. Ken has hosted and produced four separate shows, including, Branding the Experience, Cool Culture Corner, The CU Business News Podcast, Public Safety Talk Radio, and Beyond the Call. His articles have appeared in many publications, including, The Credit Union Journal, Lifestyle Entrepreneur, CU Business Magazine, ABA Bank Marketing, and as one of the first category directors of the recently launched Podcast Magazine. Ken is a well sought-after Speaker and has presented during several conferences, both in-person and virtually, worldwide, including, an appearance as an "Icon of Influence" during the New Media Summit. Ken had earned a BS in Finance and an MBA in Entrepreneurship from DePaul University, as well as, a Certification in Integrated Marketing from the University of Chicago.

Website: https://www.btcinc.net/btccontent
Ken's B+C+S Book: https://www.amazon.com/Formula-Business-Success-Kenneth-Bator-ebook/dp/B00XO7BJ4C/ref=sr_1_1?s=books&ie=UTF8&qid=1434989191&sr=1-1&keywords=kenneth+bator

Kristina Servidio:
Pilot Your Own Plane

As children, we are taught that we can be anything we want to be. The formula was simple. You were to get good grades in school so that you could get into a good college. Once you graduated college with good grades, you would get a good job which would lead to getting married, having two children and the house with the pretty white picket fence. Sounds good, right?

It was a great plan in theory, but for most, that is simply not how life works. I graduated high school at the top of my class. I took all honors and AP classes. I was on the track team. I had performed with the New Jersey Ballet Company. I was a member of multiple clubs in high school. I got into a good college. I even swept scholarship night. The plan was working.

Fast forward to college, I was still getting great grades, but college was expensive and we didn't have a lot of money. The scholarship money didn't last long. It was time to take out thousands of dollars in federal and private student loans. On top of that, I was maxed out on work study hours and was working 30 hours a week from Friday-Sunday at Blockbuster trying to keep my head above water. I did everything that I was supposed to do and graduated with a Bachelors in History and a Master's in Education. The problem was that I graduated right into a recession. Get a job as a teacher they said. Teachers will always be needed they said. It will be rewarding they said. Well, they were wrong.

The jobs were not available, and those that were, wanted someone with experience. It took much longer than anyone in my generation thought it would to enter the workforce full-time for the degrees we had earned. It wasn't from a lack of trying, but that recession hit hard and the effects were long-lasting.

Alas, I finally found my teaching job. It was great for a while but it turns out that veteran teachers didn't want to learn new tricks. I was new, but I was far from inexperienced. I knew exactly what I needed to do to get my students on the path to success. My mentor hated that I didn't need her. She also hated that I refused to conform and used methods from the year I was born just because it was the way she had always done them. Much to her dismay, my students thrived that year and I was even asked to present at professional development days, but I left the district for greener pastures.

After a few years and a few different districts, I finally woke up and realized that I wasn't going to be able to make the impact I needed to make working as a school teacher. There was simply too much politics and too much red tape. I got into the profession to help students and that was a non-negotiable. I realized this in January of my last school year teaching. I was in the middle of running a marathon that I didn't have time to train for because I was so exhausted from teaching. At the height of physical exhaustion, on the last day of a 48.6 mile running challenge, in the happiest place on Earth, Walt Disney World, Servidio Education Solutions was born. I knew the only way that I would be able to affect real change was to go out on my own. I decided to take a negative situation and make it a positive one. I knew that I couldn't keep going on being exhausted and crying myself to sleep at night because I wasn't allowed to do right by special needs students and parents. I knew there was a better way. I knew that it was going to be difficult. Nobody quite understood what I was doing. People laughed at me. They expected me to fall on my face. I didn't. I knew that it was the right thing to do and failure was simply not an option.

I have been blessed because every year has been better than the last. Every year I learn more about being a better business owner and I learn more about how to better serve the parents and students that I serve.

Like most business owners, my business crumbled during the pandemic. People were scared and in person tutoring wasn't wanted for fear that we could spread the virus. Virtual tutoring wasn't wanted because parents were concerned about how much time kids were behind the screen with school already being completely online. After all, it was only supposed to be two weeks. In addition, parents were worried that they too could lose their jobs if things didn't turn around. I could have given up. I could have declared it a failure and drowned myself in self-pity. Many business owners did. I wasn't about to let my dreams be killed by a virus, though. I did not like the way the story of my life was going so I took the pen and wrote in a plot twist. I built my business back better than it was before. I surrounded myself with mentors and business owners who refused to fail no matter what life through at them.

I have had the pleasure of helping many clients learn how to pilot their own plane and turn things around as well. What adults often do not understand is that children growing up today have far more to deal with than we ever did. There are a million reasons why kids lose self-confidence and many adults don't realize it until it's too late. Some of the many reasons include parents divorcing, failing in school, working through a learning disability that your teachers, family, and peers may not understand, having your life plastered all over social media so that you can't move on from your mistakes, physical, sexual, or verbal abuse, and being overweight. These are issues that many adults can't handle, but we forget that kids deal with these issues too and need a support system. At the end of the day, you are the pilot of your own plane. If you don't like where you are headed, send the plane in a different direction.

Focus on the ability in disability

Having a learning disability is hard. You often feel like you're dumb. You don't understand why everyone else picks up material quickly while it takes you triple the amount of time and you still struggle through it. Your teachers yell at you for not paying attention. They tell you to hurry up. They compare you to your siblings and expect that you will be just as smart as they are. It's so easy to lose your Self-Worth. It's easy to think that you're not smart enough. It's easy to think that you'll never be good enough. Maybe you think you're disappointing your parents. Maybe you think you'll never get into a good college or get a good job.

How do I know all this? I take the time to talk to my clients. I don't judge them. I don't just go by what their parents or teachers say. I listen when my students tell me what they're struggling with. I listen when they tell me about their fears. I have had hundreds of clients since I have been in business and many of them have had similar experiences and fears. At least they used to have these experiences and fears. Once they started working with me and trusting me, things began to change.

Unfortunately, we aren't really taught about learning disabilities in school, and because of that, people generally don't understand that people learn in different ways. What works for you might not work for someone else. Something that is easy for me might be hard for you. Something hard for me might seem very simple to you. A learning disability just means that you learn differently. That's it. It's not bad. You're not dumb. It has no bearing on where you will end up in life.

In fact, many people with learning disabilities are actually sought out by companies because people with learning disabilities are often able to think in creative ways which us average Joes simply cannot. Many people with Dyslexia and Autism, for example, are sought out by companies who need out of the box solutions. School often teaches us that we need to conform but those with learning disabilities tend to think outside of the box to complete tasks that the average person doesn't have to think much about. Average thinking doesn't help when many companies are in a bind. Learning disabilities are actually super powers when you think about it.

Many students with learning disabilities also go on to become Entrepreneurs. Not only do they forge their own path, but they are wildly successful when they choose to do it. The majority of the world's self-made millionaires have learning disabilities. They were tired of trying to fit into a box and decided to make their own way. It is not uncommon for a frustrated special needs parent to say something along the lines of, "Don't worry. My dyslexic child will create a job for your child".

If you don't believe me, here is a list of famous and successful people who had learning disabilities:

- ➢ Walt Disney - Dyslexia
- ➢ Keira Knightley - Dyslexia
- ➢ Orlando Bloom - Dyslexia
- ➢ Michael Phelps - ADHD
- ➢ Danielle Radcliffe - Dyspraxia
- ➢ Whoopi Goldberg - Dyslexia
- ➢ Steven Spielberg - Dyslexia
- ➢ Justin Timberlake - OCD & ADD
- ➢ Richard Branson - Dyslexia
- ➢ Charles Schwab - Dyslexia
- ➢ Henry Winkler - Dyslexia
- ➢ Charles Darwin - ADHD
- ➢ Dan Aykroyd - Autism
- ➢ Robin Williams - ADHD
- ➢ Susan Boyle - Autism
- ➢ Daryl Hannah - Autism

Clearly, a learning disability is just a hurdle to overcome on the way to greatness. As with anything else in life, how you react to it is more important than what happens to you. When you are diagnosed with a learning disability, you have a choice to make. You can allow it to define you and hold you back. Or you can choose to see it as an opportunity. Yes, it means you have to work harder in school. Yes, it may be more difficult. You also get to learn more lessons that most others don't until later in life. You get to utilize your creativity. You get to learn about perseverance. You learn to implement processes and procedures that will serve you well later in life. You also learn about compassion because you know that others are struggling just like you. You have the opportunity to help them so they don't make the same mistakes that you did.

Get behind the wheel and start guiding the plane to where you want it to go. If you need help, ask your Co-Pilot or someone on your crew. Remember that your team is there to support you in any way that you need. You just have to tell them what is going on and ask for help so that they can help you get to your destination. The journey won't always be smooth. You're bound to hit some turbulence and occasionally get caught in a storm. It happens to the best pilots. Your crew is there to help you weather the storm and make sure that you land safely at your destination.

Don't Allow Yourself to be a Victim

There are a million reasons to give up hope and wallow in self-pity. It's so simple to think that because life dealt you a bad hand, you can just throw in the towel and not live up to your full potential. What people tend not to realize is that we have to go through the bad times so that we can appreciate the good ones. After all, there is nothing better than the sunshine after the rain, or looking at that beautiful rainbow after the storm has passed. We have a ton of fun making snowmen and beautiful snow angels but the winter storm has to dump the snow first.

Recently, a client with multiple learning disabilities received a disturbing email from his teacher. Apparently, she had meant to send the email to another teacher, who was a friend of hers, instead. This email was heartbreaking to read and quite frankly, I don't understand why anyone would write it in the first place. I have changed names throughout for privacy reasons. The letter is as follows:

"I can't stand having Evan in my class. He is so lazy. I don't know how many times I need to give him the instructions so that he will do the assignments. They are clearly posted in google classroom. Any idiot can figure it out. It's not like I give these kids difficult assignments anyway.

Kids like him are so entitled. He thinks that just because he has an IEP, he can do whatever he wants. He expects extra time on his work and for me to constantly modify his assignments for him. He can't even figure out how to breakdown projects to get them submitted on time.

He knows that all he has to do is complain to his parents and he will get whatever he wants. I'm just so tired of the laziness. This was never okay when we were kids. When does it end?"

For starters, I think anyone reading this email would be incredibly offended. It's one thing to suspect that your teachers don't like you or talk about you behind your back, but it's quite another to be handed proof on a silver platter. The other issue is that this child legitimately has learning disabilities. He is anything but lazy. He has ADHD and has trouble focusing in class. It is not something that is within his control. Those modifications she was complaining about are in his IEP. They were put in place after extensive diagnostic testing. They were put in after having meetings with teachers, parents, and the child study team. These are things that he needs to help him succeed in class. These are things that many special needs kids need to succeed in class. This child could have read this and chosen to end his life. Trust me, there are many people out there who have done so. He could have read this and decided that he was dumb and was never going to amount to anything. What we talk about all the time though is how we get to choose to react. So, what did he do?

Well, for starters, with the thought of how others may react in the future if this happened to them instead of him, he forwarded the email to his parents and said that although he was okay, he wanted to do something about the situation. He knew it wasn't right what she did. He was emotionally mature enough to realize that her life must be really sad for her to have nothing better to do than talk badly about her students behind their backs. He also feared that if this was sent to someone else who didn't have the same mindset that he did, there could be catastrophic consequences. As such, he scheduled a meeting with the principal and his parents. He wanted the teacher to learn her lesson and not be able to do this to other kids. It was clear that she didn't understand his learning disabilities. Moreover, it was clear that she did not respect her students. That was a tough pill to swallow. Kids are supposed to be able to trust their teachers. They are supposed to help them learn and grow and help them achieve their dreams.

This teacher, thanks to my client, is no longer working for the school. The principal chose to address the issue and make sure that this would not happen again to anyone in his school. He decided to get teachers professional development on special education. He decided that teachers would not only need to learn more about special needs for themselves and to inform their teaching, but they would need to be able to talk to their students about special needs and that people learn differently and there is nothing wrong with that.

This situation opened up a much-needed conversation in the community about how fair does not mean equal. Every student deserves to feel safe when they go to school. They deserve to be challenged at a level that is appropriate for them. They deserve to be treated as people. They deserve the right to make mistakes so that they can learn from them. This was only possible because my client would not allow the plane to spiral downward when he received that email. He could have let it take a nose dive. He could have taken down the passengers and the crew with him. We all know that it happens. There have been far too many school shootings over the years and many of the shooters were students who were wronged in one way or another.

He didn't want to be that kind of pilot though. He knew that he could land the plane safely and get out of the storm. He gathered his crew for support. They kept the passengers calm. He called the tower and together, they all landed the plane safely.

Make Lemonade Out of Lemons

Sometimes, things happen in life that you just can't prepare for. Losing a loved one is hard whether you know it's coming or not. What we often don't talk about with children is that losing a loved one doesn't always mean death. We definitely lose them to things like heart attacks and cancer and most recently, Covid. We also lose people to car crashes and fires. Sometimes, we can prepare for it, but it usually hurts watching people suffer when we know it's coming. Other times, we are blindsided and don't get the chance to say goodbye. Either way, it takes its toll.

What about when a loved one walks out on you? What happens when they choose a vice over you? What do you do when your parent cares more about their significant other or drugs or alcohol? What happens if they just walk out on your family completely? These things happen more than the average person cares to admit. You can do everything right and still have your life turned upside down. One person's actions absolutely has the ability to send your life tumbling into chaos. It's so simple to think that it was somehow your fault. If only you were smarter, or better, or whatever, it wouldn't have happened. It's simply not true. Once again, this is where people come to a fork in the road and have to make a difficult decision. Do you wallow in self-pity? You're certainly entitled to. None of these situations are easy for an adult to handle, let alone a child. Do you let something tragic and sad define your life or do you use it as fuel to chase after your dreams and make something for yourself?

Obviously, some go down the wrong path. Some self-medicate with food or drugs. Some engage in destructive behaviors. Some will end up getting themselves killed, becoming drug addicts, or landing themselves in prison. Others simply see these events as extreme turbulence. It's really hard to fly through and it's really scary. For safety reasons, the entire crew can't always band together to help out. The pilot has to make a decision to rely on his training and calmly fly the plane into calmer skies or make a safe landing at a nearby airport.

There will always be obstacles. There will always be people who try to make you feel that you are unworthy. There will always be people who will hate on your success. Only you can make the choice is to ignore them. Only you have the power to squash the negative thoughts that pop into your head.

If you look hard enough, you will find people like you. You will find mentors who truly care about you. You will find like-minded people who want to see you succeed. There will be plenty of turbulence along the way. You'll have to hire and fire crew members throughout the journey. You may learn that the people you thought would cheer for you are actually working against you. You may find that people who were strangers on the internet end up being your biggest cheerleaders. That's ok. That's life. Nobody has all the answers. Nobody has it together all the time. Social media is a giant highlight reel. Very few people are showing their struggles, but what most successful people will tell you is that they were grateful for the rock bottom moments. In those moments where it felt like everything was lost, there is nowhere to go but up. As Gary Vaynerchuk is known for saying, he credits his ability to be a serial Entrepreneur because there was no pressure on him. His grades were awful. Nobody expected anything from him. He had the freedom to create without judgment.

No matter what is happening in your life, realize that it won't always be this way. The popular kids eventually lose their popularity. If what you are going through right now won't matter in five years, don't lose any sleep over it now. No matter how bad you think you've messed up, you can still come back from it. There have been people imprisoned multiple times for dumb mistakes that finally learned their lesson and built multi-million-dollar businesses.

The biggest key to Self-Worth and success is believing that you are worthy and that you can do it, because you can. I won't tell you it's easy to believe in yourself. I won't tell you it's easy to chase your dreams and make them a reality. I will tell you that it's worth it. I will tell you that every mistake that you make is an opportunity to learn a lesson and do better next time. I will tell you that your dream crew is out there and they're waiting for you to find them even if you have to hire and fire many crewmembers before that happens. I will tell you that you have the power to fly your own plane. You just have to decide to accept your role as the pilot. The journey won't always be smooth, but it will be worth it!

<u>BIO</u>

Kristina Servidio, Owner of Servidio Education Solutions, helps students strive for excellence in their academic careers by providing effective academic and training curricula to help bolster their studies in school. She believes in giving students the advantages they need to succeed. Kristina is recognized for her work with Orton-Gillingham, Touch Math, reading comprehension strategies, as well as the writing process. Kristina develops and implements courses, workshops, and tutoring curricula in financial literacy, study skills, career services, and college preparation and application. When not helping others achieve their goals, she can be found at Disney or planning Disney vacations for others as a Travel Planner.

Website: www.servidioeducationsolutions.com

Christine T. Rose: *Why CEOs and Leader's Self-Worth Leads To Effective, Innovative Businesses*

Leaders are often so engrossed in work or net worth that, to their own peril, they fail to address personal growth or self-worth. Countless people rise to leadership positions based on the effectiveness of the teams they have managed. Lack of Self-Worth hinders leadership effectiveness.

Meet Harry Dana, a person plagued by low Self-Worth who's just snagged a key leadership role. Any resemblance of characters or details in this fictional tale to real people or businesses are completely accidental. Whether during your first read through or later, take time to work through the coaching questions to get the greatest benefit from this chapter.

Harry Dana & NewZone Software Company

After a recent acquisition, the global software giant AllComm phased out Harry Dana's job. Though a nice severance package positioned him financially for retirement, Harry was driven to increase his already significant net worth, *"If I'm not working, I'll be worthless,"* he mused.

Coach yourself:
- ➤ Where does worth come from?
- ➤ What worth do your employees or team members have?
- ➤ What worth do newborns have?
- ➤ What worth do the elderly have when they're no longer able to work?
- ➤ Do all the employees in your company have equal worth?

WHY CEO'S & LEADER'S SELF-WORTH LEADS TO EFFECTIVE, INNOVATIVE BUSINESSES

As a high-level Manager, Harry received the benefit of working with an Executive Coach for 18 months at $1000 per month. *"What a waste of time and money,"* Harry thought, *"They should've offered a cash bonus."* After months of working with his coach rehearsing and reading up on prospective employers, Harry started feeling confident of his performance in interviews.

Seventeen months to the date of his layoff, local privately held NewZone Software hired Harry as its CEO, for 75% of his prior salary. When stock options vested in 12 months, he'd be at 85%, with a real opportunity to grow his assets if NewZone went public.

"It took my whole life, but I've finally made it." Harry grinned. *"Won't take long to catch up with Dick's net worth."* Harry's older brother Dick and he had been competing as long as he could remember.

Coach yourself:
> ➢ Where do I get my confidence?
> ➢ How much preparation is required for me to be confident?
> ➢ How have past relationships impacted my confidence?
> ➢ What drives me?
> ➢ What is enough?

The NewZone board welcomed Harry with hope and a watchful eye. They'd fired their second CEO after software problems caused the loss of several customers. Harry had the technical know-how to turn things around.

"Great to meet you Mr. Dana," Harry's executive assistant Sondra said, shaking his hand firmly.

"Great to meet you, Sandy." She didn't correct him. Harry had Sondra schedule meetings with each board member, each product lead, the VP of Sales and Marketing, and VP of Ops. Unable to quickly process and respond to all the information coming his way, imposter syndrome hit Harry like a lead brick. *"You're in way over your head, stupid,"* his inner critic taunted.

The idea of reaching out to a few former coworkers for advice flashed across his mind. Instead, Harry requested weekly reports from products, sales and marketing, finance, and operations, thinking, *"I can read everything I need to know."*

Coach yourself:
- What do I know about people I work with?
- What are their names? What do they care about? What are their goals?
- Can I admit publicly to not knowing?
- How safe do I feel asking for help?
- Where do I go for help? Who's in my corner?
- What expertise do I need to lead others?
- What are the missing conversations that I'm not having with those I lead?
- What impact do my decisions have on those I'm leading?
- What does my inner critic say?

Team leaders put in overtime to generate the requested reports. Harry shut his door, the only way he got any work done at AllCom, and read. At 11 PM the second Monday on the job, shutting down his laptop for the night, his mind wandered back to his childhood…

Dick had bullied him mercilessly. If other children were invited to their home, they were Dick's age. Harry was excluded from their games, or the brunt of their pranks. Dick's taunts still rang between his ears: *"Get outta here, stupid. Shut up. Don't be a crybaby. Nobody cares. You're a loser. You can't do anything right."*

Harry's dad, Tom, a "road warrior" in sales and an alcoholic, was either traveling, or glued to the TV. Harry remembered tugging his dad's sleeve to ask a question or show him a school project he was especially proud of:

"Dammit, Janet, get these rug rats off me!" his dad hollered.

"Just ignore him, Tom…Harry! Don't interrupt!" his mom chided.

Dick threatened Harry with more bruises. *"Nobody cares, dumbass!"* his brother told him any time he tried to challenge the status quo. Harry's mom sided with Dick's stories about any conflict. She let Harry fend for himself, rarely disciplining the boys.

Coach yourself:
- ➢ What did I tell myself when my needs went unmet?
- ➢ What messages did I receive from others?
- ➢ How many have I internalized?

> ➢ How might internalized messages be influencing my Self-Worth?
> ➢ How safe is it for me to feel included?
> ➢ How safe is it for my team members to feel welcomed and included, even if they're different in some way from other team members?
> ➢ How safe is it to challenge the status quo?

By age ten, Harry, the mule, rode his bike to the store to buy Dick's candy. By middle school, Harry resold candy at school for a profit. Harry eschewed treats himself to save money, *"I can beat Dick at saving."*

He graduated high school with a 2.5 GPA and was accepted into State University. His dad, a college dropout, said, *"Don't waste your time with college, son. You're not that smart. Just go get a job."*

Coach yourself:
> ➢ How safe is it for me to learn?
> ➢ How do I model learning safety for my team?
> ➢ How safe do I feel contributing ideas?
> ➢ How does my Self-Worth impact my behavior when others contribute thoughts or ideas?
> ➢ What are my beliefs about work and Self-Worth?
> ➢ What, if anything, does my education contribute to my Self-Worth?

> ➤ How do I celebrate my successes? My
> teams' successes?

Harry's mind wandered back to his early and mid-career roles. Eventually, he'd put himself through college, found a job in computer science, earned an MBA, married, and was promoted to managing a team. Leading small, manageable projects, Harry's technical knowledge allowed him to deliver projects on time within budget. He spent evenings and weekends chained to his computer, resentfully redoing subordinates' work. He got little satisfaction out of parenting, feeling inadequate to understand his kids' needs. Meaningful conversations with the kids or wife were rare. Now they were grown and gone, and he was divorced.

"Water under the bridge," Harry muttered to himself at midnight, his alarm set for 6 AM.

"How the hell do half of the board get to the club for a 5 AM workout? Maybe when my investment account recovers, I'll invest in a personal trainer," Harry thought, drifting off to sleep.

Coach yourself:
> ➤ How does self-worth impact my ability to
> stay mindful and present, in the moment?
> ➤ How has my self-worth impacted my
> personal relationships?
> ➤ How does my self-worth influence my
> decisions about how to use personal time?
> ➤ How does my self-worth influence my
> thoughts and habits around self-care?

Back at work, while Harry gained familiarity with product challenges, he didn't arrive early to meetings to learn about team members, or keep his office door open. He mistook friendly smiles of his Ops and Sales & Marketing VPs, who were overlooked for the CEO role. At Harry's first board meeting, he had no strategies to solidify relationships, either with his VPs, or with key customers. Harry offered an accurate technical analysis of product failures, and first steps the software teams needed to make to start recovering, but no timeline for changes. He hadn't yet connected with the software development teams to estimate how long changes would take, cost, or whether they would satisfy customers. Harry was still waiting for accounting to finalize a revised organizational budget as sales had fallen significantly over the past two quarters.

After Monday's board meeting, Sondra asked Harry if he'd like help planning or getting communications out for an all-hands meeting,

"Why are you trying to undermine me by taking critical time away from our biggest problems with wasteful socializing?" Harry asked accusingly. "Wait until we have a reason to celebrate. Stick to correspondence and calendaring, Sandy."

"Mr. Dana, as I told you, it's Sondra." Harry excused himself, closing the office door, wondering "…. God, do I *really* need to do an all-hands meeting? Those ridiculous rah-rah sessions are a complete waste of time."

Coach yourself:

- ➢ How does my Self-Worth limit my view of others' actions or words?
- ➢ How does my Self-Worth impact my ability to form and keep relationships?
- ➢ Does my Self-Worth influence my view of the offers of help I make to others?
- ➢ How does my Self-Worth influence my view of others' offers of help or support to me?
- ➢ How does Self-Worth impact my view of communication with people? Personally? At work?

Tuesday, Sondra knocked on Harry's door. "Mr. Dana, sorry to interrupt. I'm heading out to lunch with Nancy. You haven't responded to her email about a press release. Nancy has been waiting for over two weeks for your verbiage. She's not sure how long to hold off on issuing a release."

Harry looked up. "Nancy? Oh, that's right, she did send an email earlier. Set up a meeting with her for me tomorrow morning at 8."

"Mr. Dana, as we discussed at last week's meeting, Nancy job shares with John in Communications, so she's not here Wednesday. Would you like to meet with John, who is here Wednesday and Thursday? Or would you rather hold off until Monday when Nancy returns?"

Auto-pilot and the AllCom protocol for communications kicked in. "Since Nancy is initiating the conversation, Monday's fine." Harry answered, absentmindedly, still half lost in thought about software fixes.

"Are you sure Mr. Dana? Our community of private owners are waiting, and the Business Journal prints tomorrow, so it would need to go out by 3 PM today."

Harry realized he'd failed to see the urgency of the matter, or even to consider what owners would want. Embarrassed, he barked "You handle it. Write up something for me to review this afternoon, I'll approve it, and you can send it to Nancy."

"Sure," Sondra, replied, shaking her head no, and closing the door behind her. Sondra emailed him at 2 PM. Nancy followed up at 2:15, and Sondra told her, "Mr. Dana hasn't responded with the information you requested. He is still in his office with the door closed." Nancy forwarded the press release status to John before leaving for the weekend. He could handle it.

Forgetting all about the press and the shareholders, Harry spent the rest of the week finalizing his brilliant solutions to NewZone's software problems. With support from NewZone's product leadership team they could accomplish so much. He had Sondra set up a meeting Friday afternoon with NewZone's three product leads, Ashton, Jack, and Stuart.

After a few minutes of small talk, Harry had a field day ripping into the technical failures of each of NewZone's three major software products, missing the ashen look on Jack's face, the redness in Stuart's cheeks, Ashton's crossed arms and how she nearly pushed her chair into Harry's office window, creating an extra two feet of distance between her and the new CEO. Harry had all the solutions. His only questions were whether their teams had the competence to make the changes, how much it would cost, how long it would take to get new releases out, and how soon they could get started with his fixes.

Harry stood up and extended his hand, "Jack, Stuart and Ashley, thank you for your time and cooperation. I'm looking for project timelines for new product releases to be in my office Monday at 8 AM. Have a great weekend."

Awkward silence followed as none of the three accepted his extended hand. Rather, they skirted the table and Harry on their way out the door. Harry felt it was a productive meeting and they'd come around to see he was saving them all a great deal of work.

"Sondra, excellent week," Harry commented, leaving at 4:55 PM, satisfied with his solutions to NewZone's product failures and the meeting with Jack and Stuart and the woman lead. He was ready to relax for the first time since he started at NewZone.

Coach yourself:
- ➢ What blind spots am I missing because of Self-Worth gaps?
- ➢ Which of my strengths may become weaknesses without awareness?
- ➢ How does my Self-Worth impact my ability to balance multiple or competing priorities?
- ➢ How does my Self-Worth limit my ability to empathize with others?

> ➢ How does my Self-Worth impact my ability to relate to those of different ages or genders, ethnicities, belief systems, sexual orientations, or physical abilities?

On Monday at 7:50 AM, Harry headed past Sondra into the boardroom for an 8 AM meeting. Harry sat in the boardroom reflecting on his success, feeling rested for the first time in months. At 8:05, Alex, the board president, stepped briskly into the boardroom and closed the door.

"Harry, the board met Saturday morning. We're letting you go with six months' salary, which is more than generous. Your unvested stock remains with NewZone. You're a brilliant software strategist with high integrity, but you're not a fit for NewZone."

Harry stammered, "But Alex…I've just solved NewZone's most significant technical problems! I expected a bonus."

"Harry, we need a CEO who can lead our people. AllComm's and NewZone's leadership styles don't align. We appreciate your work documenting your solutions for our product leads. We wish you the best."

She smiled and shook his hand before striding out of the boardroom. Harry felt a strange mix of irritation and relief. Quietly, he gathered his few items and headed home, ready for a new chapter.

Coach yourself:
> ➢ When do I feel most satisfied?
> ➢ What fuels my sense of Self-Worth?

> ➢ Is my current role in alignment with my knowledge, skills, passion, and gifts?
> ➢ Am I leading to gain Self-Worth, or to offer it to those I serve?
> ➢ How does my Self-Worth impact my ability to speak with care and candor?
> ➢ How will I grow my Self-Worth?
> ➢ What would be a positive story ending?

Here's one possibility: NewZone hires an excellent CEO with high Self-Worth. Harry's happily consulting at a larger organization. Still trying to one-up Dick, but working on Self-Worth.

<u>BIO</u>

Christine Rose helps owners of SMEs grow leadership, effective teams, and profitable businesses. Award-winning ICF-ACC, Business Coach, Certified Value Builder Advisor, Certified Psychological Safety Coach, and member of Forbes Coaches Council, Christine's insights are featured on Forbes.com, Public Interest Radio and National Business Radio. She is Co-Author of the #1 International Bestseller, ***Cracking the Rich Code, Vol. 4***, and Author of the *Amazon #1 New Release,* ***Life Beyond #MeToo: Creating a Safer World for Our Mothers, Daughters, Sisters & Friends,*** featured in the U.N. Foundation.

Website: www.coachchristinerose.com

Pat Roque: *How A Box Of Rocks Saved My Life: Celebrate Why YOU Rock!*

They call me the Rock Star Leadership & Career Transformation Coach, but not because I've got a big ego. In fact, it's just the opposite. It turns out that my gift (as I learned after a midlife meltdown) is helping awesome professionals rediscover their zone of genius.

Together, we channel their inner rock star as thought leaders in their industry to gain the rewards and recognition that they deserve.

My father's name was Rocky. My father in law's name was Rocky. My favorite movie of all time was the Best Picture of 1976...Rocky. I'm Italian and love marble and granite....and I married a handsome Cuban, Alex, almost 30 years ago, so now my married name is Roque (which, as you can imagine, means "rock" in Spanish).

My mom, also named Pat, is a retired Nurse who calls me her resilient cat with 9 lives. It feels like every time S*it hits the fan and life throws me a giant curveball, she'll say the same old, "I never worry about you because you always land on your feet," with a mom-like proud grin. Naturally, that loving remark also makes me sigh as I keep pressing my luck and forging ahead, trying to forever pick up the pieces and super glue my life and career back together. It feels kind of like Humpty Dumpty and Gorilla glue, to be honest. I promise you that's not the deal I signed up for. The road to resilience can become quite exhausting.

When my daughter, Lindsey, now a Doctor of Audiology at Johns Hopkins University and Medical Center, said I was built to lead others through the pandemic, it suddenly dawned on me that they were *both* right.

Why?

Navigating change comes naturally to me, thanks to lots of practice. Like you, I've had more than my share of career and life challenges over the years, but I simply refuse to let obstacles stop me. Instead, when God closes one door, it's time to climb through the window.

For those of you who only see me on Good Morning America, featured in Cosmopolitan Magazine, or other media around the world, you might think success looks easy, but I promise you it's surely not...it's simply that I'm committed to getting one step better every day. Inch by inch. One foot in front of the other. One stepping stone, one rock at a time.

Pivot #1:

At age 23, I was an overachieving agency publicist who was the passenger in a seemingly innocent car accident and put my head through the windshield. When the head injury lingered and I wasn't well enough to return to my job, my boss wisely said, "Hang a shingle, and I'll hire you."

God chose, and I listened. I heard the calling to do things differently. We just celebrated 33 years since I became an Entrepreneur with my shiny new consultancy called, Business Boomers. It was born with a milk crate, a recycled desk, and old typewriter in my bedroom at my parents' house. I was raised in the poorest immigrant town in one of the wealthiest counties in the country. No silver spoon, no summer camp, or fancy anything. Since my dad was one of 12 kids, my two brothers and sister and I had many dozens of cousins and lots of laughs and love. We wore hand-me downs, walked home from school singing with our heavy bookbags in tow, played out in the fields like the Little Rascals (only coming home for 5:30 prompt dinner). My parents were pillars of our community.

Mom is now the matriarch of our entire Nunno family, and was always the one everyone called whenever they needed help or medical advice. She retired after 30+ years of nursing, and still engages on Facebook daily as she lovingly stalks her grandkids, nieces and nephews who think she's the funniest "techno grandma" ever. Yes, she has a new laptop, wears an Apple Watch, and can facetime on her iPhone. No joke. At age 89, she's sweet and funny and wildly proud of my success. She chimes in on my Facebook Live streams whenever she can and enjoyed the family Zoom gatherings during the pandemic.

My Dad was a character, to say the least. Bigger than life, literally and figuratively. He was a retired Police Officer, then ran the civil division of our county courthouse for 30+ years. When he retired from civil service, my first (unpaid, of course) gig was to help get him elected to city council. Of course, he won, and went onto to become a Housing Commissioner, and serve on several boards. I earned my first board of director's seat leading our Public Library. Dad used to say, "Make sure you challenge every 5th or 7th item...make them stay on their toes and know that someone is closely watching where the money was being spent."

I remember he once begged me to put him to work. He showed up one day at my new office with a brown paper lunch bag asking when his breaks would be. I had to leave for a TV show guest appearance that day. While I was on the set, rumor has it he yelled at my callers, "Why are you on the phone instead of watching my beautiful daughter on TV?" He was fired the next day.

Dad's obesity haunts me daily, as I'm secretly afraid of the "Nunno curse" as his weight wore out his heart and he died at age 70. He's been gone 20 years now and I still laugh at how he would try to pretend he supported my entrepreneurship...but every year or so would ask when I was getting a "real job." (More on that later...)

We didn't see eye to eye on how to earn a living. He landed me a government job doing publicity at the racetrack and I lasted a month. It was super boring and I spent every night being harassed by the gambling old men as I interviewed owners in the winner's circle and worked with the media. Sorry, no thanks. Sometimes, success is learning what you do not like...and pivoting quickly.

Even at that young age, I knew enough to listen to the inner voice telling me key lessons:

➢ Don't ever let people disrespect you; you deserve better

➢ Appearances don't show the whole story

➢ Embrace your strengths and find work that makes your heart sing, helping others, and making an impact

Although, now that I see my brother Mike comfortably retired at age 60, on the days when I'm burnt out, I sometimes wonder (for just 5 minutes) if Dad was right. Following that inner voice, I knew that I was meant for more. It was my choice to work on other people's dreams, or to create a legacy and build my own.

For the next 20 years, I'd work remotely as a virtual VP of Experiential Marketing (before the tech was even available). My circle of friends and colleagues included top corporate leaders, visionary business builders, and many of the top event marketers from around the world. We traveled to Special Event Conferences, training on the latest in technology, safety, innovation and engagement with folks who produced Olympic opening ceremonies, Superbowl halftime shows, the Academy Awards, and more.

I found my niche marketing to working moms as the family health and shopping quarterbacks. These "sandwich generation" professionals were often midlife warriors trying to keep all the plates spinning as they juggled caring for aging parents, kids in school, crazy careers, and trying to stay sane while remembering to have a healthy meal on the table. They were, and still are, the backbone of our country, making company and family decisions at the intersection of healthcare and luxury brands. No wonder I helped shaped interactive marketing for AT&T, Infiniti, DeBeers Diamonds, and upscale healthcare systems across the country.

Pivot #2:

Alex and I were married, had 2 amazing kids, and life was rather amazing...until my son slipped into a coma with bacterial meningitis at 13 months old. Yes, we prayed hard, and drove the doctors and school system crazy as diehard advocates.

That special needs family is a "club" that we didn't sign up for, with no roadmap to follow. We had hundreds of therapy sessions over many years. Meanwhile, my dad suffered with six long years of major heart disease before he passed (the month after my sitter quit with zero warning).

Yes, I empathize with the struggles of working moms in what we call the "Sandwich Generation" where overburdened leaders juggle work, teams, and crazy family dynamics. In fact, I worked on an Emmy-Award winning documentary with some of the hottest newscasters in our day called, "You and Your Aging Parents." Yet somehow, I managed to keep the business afloat, marketing for health and luxury brands with amazing results, and we never had an unpaid bill. However, the long days turned into longer nights and weekends. I thought about looking for a salaried job with predictable hours. It became overwhelming with my family obligations, and no company was looking for a marketing leader with such a heavy personal burden. Workplace flexibility was not yet "a thing" and yet I was surely not the only one feeling the pressure. This was before Family Leave Act, Americans with Disabilities, and other legal protections meant to give overworked moms like me a chance to contribute in the salaried workforce. I just didn't fit their 9-to-5, in office model.

Instead, I built strong collaborative partnerships with talent folks who I trusted. Together, we co-marketed our services and covered each other's backs to allow us to manage whatever hit the fan. Within my company, we shifted from the craziness of an event marketing model to a more predictable daytime routine, serving as the virtual VP of Marketing Communications on retainer. That model worked well. Our team and clients were amazing, and decades later, we are still grateful for their support and friendship.

Pivot #3

When Steven finally tested out of special education at age 11, his newfound intellect became its own struggle; the system didn't know how to help families with extreme gifts and special needs, all rolled into one funny kid. He played lacrosse, became an Eagle Scout, graduated college, and now lives his dream job as the youngest News Director at NBC-TV in Myrtle Beach. Thank goodness for hair dye, or I'd be gray many years ago. Steven is a miracle; he's our biggest triumph over adversity, and we're so proud.

When it was time to move up, Alex and I decided to earn our Master's degrees in Organizational Leadership together (online, of course). We participated in a fabulous cohort program at Thomas Edison University and published our thesis on best practices for virtual teams in Spring 2001 BEFORE 9/11 made remote work a necessity for so many. Yes, we're always ahead of the curve!

I put my business aside and spent the next 10 years driving great results as partner to healthcare, pharma, luxury and women's brands on behalf of top global agencies like WPP, Interpublic Group, WebMD, and EveryDay Health.

Ironically, we plan and God laughs. Historically I'm an over-achiever and the go-to person teams count on for honest input, and stellar results. Yet, somehow, the better I performed, it felt like the faster my roles disappeared. I was fired, more than once.

When I detected actions that contradicted my values and morals, it quickly became time to move on. I have ZERO poker face and only work with people and companies who insist on integrity. In fact, when a former manager reprimanded me for, "caring too much about the clients instead of excess inventory we had to sell," I knew it was time to move on. Another manager warned me that, after closing a $2.4 million dollar sale (the largest in the company's history, with his support and blessing) that we'd likely have to, "pack our bags and leave because we may not have the ability to delivery on our order." Really? Are you kidding? My reputation means everything, and we immediately planned an exit strategy because I can't work for liars or thieves. Sorry, not sorry. No regrets, just hard-earned learnings. More than once.

Pivot #4: My Mess Became My Message

When a phone call revealed my employer lost our funding and my role was eliminated, I had an ugly, snot-crying meltdown that lasted two years. It was bad. Really bad. My antidepressant medication backfired and I'd truly hit rock bottom. Like so many, I spent ridiculous hours applying for jobs that would have put me back feeling like I had to sell my soul and sacrifice my family to keep them happy.

It was then, at my 50th birthday, that my best friend, Rose, refused to sit by and watch me spin out of control. So, she created the best birthday gift ever: this miraculous box that says, "50 ROCKS and so do you." It's filled with 50 things that are special about me....and it sparked the rebranding and redirection from marketing only companies to truly helping their teams and leaders thrive in their zone of genius as well. (Visit my 50 ROCKS blog to learn more.)

The Rock On Success System was born, and we haven't looked back except to say THANK YOU for the bumps and bruises. Today, we're skillfully empowering leaders and their teams to shine, unapologetically, and celebrate why they ROCK. We've built a thriving team of top-notch talent who are Subject Matter Experts in the hottest topics you and your team need to not just survive, but truly thrive. We're seeing the "new normal" as a game-changing opportunity to reset and breathe new life into challenges that we may have tried to ignore for too long. No more empty promises; our clients are stepping up and putting their resources into driving lasting change in productivity, diversity and belonging, and more. We're here to help you find clarity, confidence, upleveled communication, and nurture masterful connections that bring momentum to move forward.

My MESS became our MESSAGE, and we'll ride out this sea change together. *Your transformation* starts right now, too.

<u>BIO</u>

Pat Roque and her Rock On Success System helps leaders and their organizations rock their leadership potential as they gain the clarity, confidence, communication and connection skills to leverage their contributions, uplevel their skills, articulate their value, and feel respected and fulfilled as part of a thriving in-person, hybrid, or virtual team...despite unsettling times.

Leveraging 20+ years as a communications and PR expert with top firms, Pat's acclaimed executive training and strength-based workshops drive collaboration, engagement, and productivity through her tested and proven framework of signature systems.

Whether meeting 1:1, in group coaching or from the stage, her audiences gain confidence, leadership effectiveness, career fulfillment and a rock-solid future. She's a fierce advocate for strength-based culture, radical flexibility and workplace unification, women's leadership, diversity and belonging at organizations including WebMD, Bayer, SHRM, HBA, Novartis, & KPMG. She's an avid golfer and teaches networking on and off the golf course.

Pat's team and her system offer a breath of fresh air: call on Pat to drive metrics that matter, yet offer more fun and fulfillment than you've had in a long time!

Website: https://rockonsuccess.com/

LinkedIn: https://www.linkedin.com/in/patroque

8

Jean Krisle: Celebrating The Miracle Of 10,000 Beds, Inc: *How A Mother's Hope & Determination Rocked The Addiction & Recovery Industry*

Oh, the stories you'll hear; just ask anyone what a company called "10,000 Beds" might do and the answers will range from mattress sales to truck beds. Sometimes, the story happens while you are filling your gas tank in Las Vegas and a gentleman just keeps staring at your license plate (which reads "10000Beds") and finally walks over and says, "I can't figure out what 10,000 Beds means, unless you're a madam at one of the Nevada brothels!?" You just can't make this stuff up (I am still laughing over this one, five years later!). These past 7 years with 10,000 Beds have brought immeasurable joy mixed with sadness, but the people we've met and the stories we've heard have changed us to the core. Some made us laugh, some made us cry, but all left an imprint on our hearts.

I've never been a drinker and I've never used an illegal drug. When my school mates were experimenting with marijuana at parties, I was sipping a Coke and eating at our local pizza joint. When I did drink alcohol (all 3 times), I had a rum and Coke or a red wine. The one time I drank too much in college, I found myself unintentionally sliding through a mud puddle near the dorms and miserably bent over a commode soon thereafter. Not drinking was not a religious or moral choice at the time; I just wasn't interested. I didn't like the taste of alcohol, the loss of self-control, or the thought of making a fool of myself. Not much has changed. If only my "not interested" genes were hereditary; instead, my kids were likely born with a terrifying gene mix from an alcoholic father on my side and an alcoholic grandfather on their Dad's side, plus the co-dependent, addictive personalities of their Dad and me (addiction isn't only about substances). Thankfully, they've prevailed over this dangerous disadvantage, but not without a few skirmishes along the way.

So, my children's high school memories of attending parties are very different from my high school memories of my Mom forbidding me to go to any high school parties that a particular friend of mine wasn't attending. I was only allowed to go to the parties HE went to because she trusted him. If HE was going to be there, she believed it was an OK party. Oh, the naivete of Moms. That's how my story begins, because I am Mom to six awesome kids, and as they were growing up, I trusted them AND their friends. My mantra was, "I'll trust you until you prove me wrong, so don't prove me wrong." I am absolutely convinced that naivete is hereditary.

When you are faced with something unfamiliar and your gut tells you something is wrong, as a human, it's typical to take a "watch and wait position." We listen, we ask questions, we observe, and based on our existing knowledge, as well as our recent observations, we make a judgement call – and either our gut is right, or we have indigestion. When my life was turned upside down and we unexpectedly joined the millions of families battling addiction, I knew that even though I have a weak stomach, I did not have indigestion.

A mother's worst fear is losing a child. What does "losing a child" mean? Most often losing a child is associated with an incurable disease, death, or kidnapping; addiction rarely makes the list. The reality, however, is that **addiction is stealing our children**, and it almost took mine.

I am one of the lucky parents. My child is alive and working on recovery, but it's been a long road for all of us. This road I would gladly trek over and over to see my child healthy, happy, and free of the chains of addiction, but a rough road still and one my child will be on for the rest of their life. Addiction is not an incurable disease, but it's a disease that requires treatment, vigilance, respect, hard work, and long-suffering.

When a parent suspects their child is using drugs or drinking excessively, their first reaction is often denial, followed by a growing concern, real frustration, passive accusations, unwarranted guilt, not-so-passive anger, and finally, complete and total confusion and bewilderment compounded by outright fear. They ask themselves these questions, over and over and over:

> How can this be happening?
> What did I do wrong?
> What did we do wrong?
> Why would my child do this?
> How can we help?
> Who should we talk to?
> How can we find the right treatment program?
> Do you think my child is suicidal?
> Oh my gosh, is my child going to die?
> Who can I trust?
> And sometimes, sadly, "Oh no, what will the neighbors think?"

Daily life for the entire family becomes filled with tears, irritation, short-tempers, anxiety, depression, fear, guilt, and desperation, because it's no longer just the loved one battling addiction, it's the entire family. No one expected this, no one prepared for this, and no one has the tools or resources to deal with it.

This is what I experienced as my own adult child was battling alcoholism and addiction. We were fortunate to have more resources than many, but we had absolutely no knowledge about addiction, no personal experience to draw from, no one to ask the 7,568 questions we were juggling in our brains, and no conception of the trauma that might have occurred somewhere in the past, that has now led to our child's need to self-medicate and escape.

We were lost and scared. I was at my wit's end. From the early signs of something being wrong (sadly, not indigestion) to the realization that we were dealing with an addict with an active addiction, we experienced everything addiction brings with it – every negative and terrifying behavior possible by the addict and every enabling effort made in the name of love by me, specifically. That's right, and all in the name of love. We really were lost. I became the perfect enabling mom. I loaned money, offered housing, transported grandchildren, fed, supported, clothed, etc. I was totally naïve and unaware that anything I provided was simply funding and supporting the addiction. I didn't know any better, like so many other parents and loved ones of someone who is in active addiction. I thought that I could love my child back to sobriety, but instead, I was loving my child into a casket. I couldn't believe **my child** would lie to me, but I finally realized how easy it was for **the addict** to lie to me. What is it they say?

"An alcoholic will steal your wallet. A drug addict will steal your wallet and then help you look for it."

Over many months and many more highs and lows, we educated ourselves, we stopped enabling, and we were able to identify credible options for treatment. It was an unaccepted gift the first time, because our child was still in denial. Anger, denial, and refusal to accept the help offered were voiced clearly and loudly.

The second time, it was not our idea, it was theirs. When admission to treatment was completed, I went to work. I told myself if I was this lost, afraid, and inept at dealing with addiction at my age and with my life experience, then what was the parent going to do who didn't have the resources, experience, or education that I was so fortunate to have? I was not a young parent, and I was not without financial resources, but I couldn't stop thinking about the fact that so many are in a very different situation than I was and that their battle would be even more difficult than ours.

Here begins the story of 10,000 Beds. It wasn't news to me that families were often in denial when a family member was battling a substance use disorder, and it absolutely was not news to me that many families hid the fact from their friends and relatives. Add to these facts the lack of understanding about addiction, the fact that it's a disease resulting from (most often) unresolved, untreated trauma in someone's life. All I could think about was how much damage was being done, unintentionally, because of a prideful need to pretend everything was hunky dory when it absolutely was not. Sending your addicted child off to a "summer camp" and expecting them to return "cured" is the biggest and most damaging mistake a parent can make. I needed to learn more so I could explain this to other parents. I offered to volunteer in a treatment program. I needed to gain a better understanding of all of this. I listened in on calls asking for help. The voices were broken, to match their hearts, and I could hear the frantic desperation in their words as they asked for help – with no money, no insurance, no resources. They were 100% alone and scared. No one believed in them anymore, and they no longer believed in themselves. The family had already mortgaged their home at least once for a failed treatment experience, friends were tired of the free loading, missing items, couch surfing, and now, at this pivotal moment when this person KNEW they were going to die, KNEW they had burned every bridge that had been offered to them, and KNEW they needed and wanted help, there was no one to turn to, even the treatment programs had to say "no" because their scholarship beds were full.

In the world of addiction treatment, most treatment program owners build a percentage of scholarships into their business plan, so when these frantic calls are received, they can help. Often there is good news, but more often there is not; not because the treatment program doesn't want to help, but because they have already given out their scholarships and don't have an open scholarship bed. As I listened to the incoming calls, more than half were asking for scholarships. It was heartbreaking and so demoralizing to hear the tearful pleading voices asking for help on one end of the call and the tearful apologetic voices having to say no on the other end. It broke my heart. It broke everyone's hearts.

After several weeks of working on presentations I could make to parents, an informational brochure I could have printed, and speaking with families without resources, I realized that conversation and brochures were not what they needed. They needed scholarships for treatment for their loved one!

My career has been spent working with and for nonprofit organizations. As my heart was breaking for these families seeking help, my thoughts started swirling around in my head about how I might help. As the thoughts kept swirling, I spent quite a bit of time visiting treatment programs in Southern California and Utah, and I discovered two common denominators: 1) they cared – the owners cared, and the staff cared, and they already had a scholarship option in place, but it was usually full, and 2) they all had at least one empty bed in their facility. That's when my brain went into high gear. I wanted to help these families who could not afford treatment for their loved one, these individuals who were calling with one last hope and asking for help, and all I could think of was the at least one empty bed in EVERY facility I visited.

At this point, I was excited, I could see a solution to the need for scholarships beds, but I couldn't imagine why someone else had not already done it. I needed to make certain my idea was sound and ethical and did not cross any lines of impropriety. It was at this time I met my Founding Board Members, each one unique in their recovery and life history, and each one supportive, passionate, and brilliant!

They are still my heroes. They taught me so much about addiction, treatment, and recovery. They taught me about giving back and about courage and strength. They showed me the enormous amount of conviction and effort it takes to leave addiction behind and live a life in recovery. They were my mentors, they still are, and I love and respect them to this day. So, we talked, I learned, we created plans, shared ideas at board meetings, and carefully and strategically, moved forward. They made calls. I made calls. I spoke with owners I had met, and I asked: "If I start a 501c3 nonprofit organization with a mission to help those individuals and families who are seeking help for addiction but have NO resources, would you consider an annual donation to 10,000 Beds of at least ONE scholarship for addiction? No one turned me down.

NO ONE TURNED ME DOWN! THEY ALL SAID YES! OH MY GOSH! THEY BELIEVED IN THE MISSION OF 10,000 BEDS!

It was time to get to work, starting with the creation of the 501c3, selecting the name of 10,000 Beds, creating the logo, attending industry conferences, and talking with treatment program owners to ask for one scholarship bed per year. Once we had received a dozen or so donated scholarship beds, we opened our application process and announced it through social media. It's not a simple application, it's 40 questions and they must all be answered. It's our first qualifier to receive a scholarship. Our second is the application itself; we want to be certain they meet our criteria and truly are ready for help and have no other way to get it. Our third is what we call, Monday Check-In. We are not an overnight process; our scholarships take time, and our applicants are required to check in with us every Monday until we can find them a good program to match their unique needs.

Our 10,000 Beds scholarship applicants have come from 47 states and from all races, genders, income levels, backgrounds, and addictions. We have partnered with extraordinary treatment programs in 45 states. Each year the number of applicants has increased, and our partnerships have continued. We are fortunate to partner with a variety of programs that provide dual diagnosis and a range of modalities, serve unique populations (LGBQT, etc.), range from 45 days to 26 months in length, and/or provide a higher level of care that can support individuals with acute medical conditions on top of their substance use disorder.

In the past seven years, we have awarded nearly $20,000,000 in addiction treatment scholarships through our generous partners who have donated their scholarship beds for us to fill. This is beyond anything I ever planned or expected. We are humbled and honored to be part of this opportunity to change lives.

Although I have always been on the front line, as well as the face of 10,000 Beds, my board has always been right there to help and support, and so has my husband. I can't write one more word without recognizing the incredible support I have received from Hal Krisle. He's been there from day one and through thick and thin. When we reached a point where I could no longer handle everything, Hal jumped in and went to work! We absolutely would not be where we are today as an organization without Hal's support and hands-on work. He is ALWAYS on the front line with me.

In the past seven years, 10,000 Beds has partnered with more than 250 vetted treatment programs throughout the country. We have vetted hundreds of programs by visiting, talking, meeting, seeing with our own eyes, and getting to know the program. It's a lot of work, but so very rewarding!

After two years of rapid growth, Hal and I felt we needed to have more access to our partners, and we opted to take 10,000 Beds on the road. We sold our home, took the proceeds and added much needed funding to the 10,000 Beds budget, purchased an RV, wrapped it in the bright blue 10,000 Beds logo, and headed out on a two-year cross-country trip to provide HOPE, raise awareness, and change perceptions of addiction and recovery. With board input, we named this outreach program with a hashtag: #ontheroad4recovery. We covered more than 30,000 miles, met with thousands of individuals and families, spoke at recovery awareness rallies, art festivals, music concerts, schools, churches, and communities. Through these events, we shared our message, provided scholarships, connected with new partners, and met incredible, humble, grateful people in recovery, or not. We received the exposure we were hoping for. Everywhere we went people were waiting to have their photo taken in front of "Big Blue," our logo-wrapped RV, and they knew who we were and what we did. We couldn't have been more surprised. To say there were tears of gratitude would be an understatement. We cried, they cried, we were a connected puddle – all in the name of recovery.

On a freeway in California, a woman in the Express Lane rolled down her passenger window and waved madly. The 91-S freeway in Southern California mid-afternoon might as well be a parking lot, so her attention getting efforts were easily noticed. We assumed we had a flat tire, or there was something wrong with our truck. Hal rolled down the driver's side window and acknowledged her with a wave, and she yelled out: "I need to talk to you. I am a Probation Officer in Orange County and I've heard about 10,000 Beds!" Honestly, shock was probably our first reaction, then concern as we WERE driving on the freeway pulling 14,000 lbs. of RV behind us, and then we chuckled and Hal yelled back, "What's your email?" She hollered back her email and it was too hard to hear her, so Hal shouted out my email and told her to connect that way. She nodded, and the next day I had an email, hopefully sent from the safety of her office. A relationship developed from there and our relationships with the California, Arizona, and Utah probation departments has resulted in "treatment in lieu of incarceration" judgements for several 10,000 Beds Scholarship Applicants.

While in Ohio, we pulled into a large rest stop with a restaurant (rest stops back east are the coolest). We had been driving in a horrific rainstorm and were grateful to be off the road safely. Because our truck and RV were an extremely long combination, we pulled clear to the back of the rest stop to park. As we covered our heads and ran from the truck toward the restaurant, I saw a family also running across the parking lot. They appeared to be running to the restaurant too, but as I watched them run it was apparent that they were running NOT to the restaurant, but to us. I shouted this to Hal over the cacophony of rain and he looked over to see them closing the gap between us and them. We slowed down and they approached us, still in the middle of a downpour, and the lady said, "We just had to meet you! We saw your rig pull into the parking lot and noticed your website on the side of the RV and checked it out. We want to thank you for what you are doing!" Here we are, in the middle of Ohio where we know no one, in a non-stop flood of rain, and this family of four felt compelled to run across the parking lot through the flood of rain to meet us and say thank you. To say we were stunned would be an understatement. Before we could even respond, the Mom hugged me, and the daughter hugged Hal. The son and husband were standing back watching with smiles. It was almost surreal. Then the Mom continued, "We want to thank you because we understand the service you are providing, there is such a huge need for help. Your resource will be life saving for so many people." She added, "My husband is 17 years in recovery and my son is 17 months clean." Suddenly, this crazy moment started to make sense.

There are moments when I have time to reflect on the people we have met #ontheroad4recovery, and when I do, this family always comes to mind. Here are four people who have faced addiction – individually and as a family – and are working daily to sustain the newfound realization that they each matter and have value.

It was their sense of Self-Worth that allowed them to run across that parking lot in pouring rain with smiles on their faces to say a simple thank you. Gratitude was evident in their every word. They did not feel entitled because of their achievement or as if their challenges were over. They were realistic, humble, and grateful for sobriety and every single day they had together.

Self-Worth (sometimes called Self-Esteem) is just one facet of an ongoing, ever-changing life in recovery. Working on Self-Worth is critical to long term recovery. Individuals in recovery must value themselves enough to be willing to *do the work* that's required to stay sober and to be satisfied with themselves and their lives.

When our #ontheroad4recovery cross-country trips ended with Covid-19, we created a new way to reach out to our 10,000 Beds partners and friends through our weekly *On The Air For Recovery Podcast*. Each episode is unique; we talk about all things recovery, we talk about life, and we remind everyone that, *we are all in recovery from something - heartbreak, loss, grief, addiction, and more.* You can find us on Apple Podcasts or your favorite podcast provider.

Some might think 10,000 Beds sells mattresses, others might call me 'Madam', some say we are heroes, but they would all be wrong. 10,000 Beds is a 501c3 nonprofit organization that provides HOPE to families and individuals battling addiction, and through our scholarship program and incredible partners, provides an OPPORTUNITY for individuals seeking help to CHANGE their own lives. We are simply the connector. The individuals on their way to a life in recovery do the real work. They are the real heroes.

"We envision a world where ALL individuals in recovery from a substance use disorder – from any and all backgrounds – are not sidelined because of their past, but welcomed, embraced, and included as valuable, lovable people with limitless futures."— Jean Krisle, Founder, 10,000 Beds, Inc.

<u>BIO</u>

A courageous and charismatic leader, consistent influencer, and innovative socialpreneur, Jean founded and continues to lead 10,000 Beds, a 501c3 nonprofit organization now in its 7th year of operation. Building from a desire to support the many individuals without resources seeking help for a substance use disorder, Jean's creation of 10,000 Beds, Inc., a life-changing and inspirational force in the addiction & recovery community and the only nationwide 501c3 awarding nearly $20,000,000 in DONATED addiction treatment scholarships from vetted treatment programs across the country, is nothing short of a miracle. As a former Vice President of Communications for an international organization based in Washington DC and a master connector of for-profit corporations and non-profit organizations, Jean has an insider's view of corporate America as well as lifetime of experience in the not-for-profit sector.

Jean is married to her partner and husband, Hal Krisle. Together they share 11 children, 33 grandchildren, and 2 great-grandchildren. Jean and Hal currently reside in Cedar City, UT.

Shout out to our 10,000 Beds Founding Board Members: Kristina Steele, Aaron Earnest, Terry Patton, Kymberly Lynd, and Johnny Grab. Every one of them a hero. I am forever grateful.

Website: https://10000beds.org/
Podcast: https://podcasts.apple.com/us/podcast/on-the-air-for-recovery/id1554411242

Michael Merritt:
Progress = Happiness

We are all born to succeed and we need to grow Spiritually, Mentally, and Physically each day. As we progress each day, we will transform our lives and increase our worth and value to not only ourselves, but to others.

Let's begin our transformation starting with our mindset and continuing with Self-Esteem, goals, and taking action. The kingdom mindset starts with your heart and spirit. It is the conscious decision that everyone makes to live a better, more purposeful life. You are in charge of your mind, not the other way around. What happens in all of our minds starts when we are born. What were the mindsets of your role models and influences? What things were said to you when you were growing up that were positive or negative, and which ones did you hold on to?

All of these things begin to set your mind in a certain direction. Then, life goes on until we learn better coping skills and tools to go from stuck to unstuck. As we grow, we get more feedback. Many times, this will determine our mindset, depending on whether that is positive or negative, especially if we are not intentional with our thoughts. Who are you listening to? If we listen to the wrong people, they can have a negative impact on our lives. At times, people do not understand what they are saying with their words or actions because they don't consider or know your history. Matter of fact, there are just mean people in the world. All of it sets our mind one way or another.

It is time to put a stop to the old thoughts which are not uplifting and positive, along with the feelings or thoughts causing you pain. Start filling yourself up with the truths about yourself like: You are a champion and you are unique. God put a purpose in your imagination for you. It's ok if no one else understands as long as it is toward positivity. God gave you the skills and talent for your purpose. The only way to start is by making the decision to change, knowing it will be uncomfortable at first. You must keep hope that it is all for your best. You are born to Succeed! Never give up!

PROGRESS = HAPPINESS

When you understand that you are a Child of God, it doesn't matter who your parents are or who said what. You know you are loved. We can't put our life into someone else's opinions. Depending on where you are in life and where you want to be rests where you have your mind set.

There are seven ways to change your mindset:

> Input (reading, watching, listening to videos, books, podcasts, audiobooks)
> Affirmations/Scriptures
> Put on the armor of God every day
> Who is your closest people of influence?
> How is your output?
> Be intentional - focus goes where energy flows
> Positive self-talk daily

It starts with the right mindset, which includes Spiritual, Mental, Physical, Faith, Hope, and Love, while using the right tactics, tools, strategies, and lastly, taking massive action. The execution of this knowledge is essential. Knowledge without implementation is useless. As the great Zig Ziglar said, "You don't have to be great to start, but you do have to start to be great."

It is a Mind that says, "I know I am strong enough; I am smart enough, pretty enough, valuable to others, I create value to this World!" We have to listen to our Inner Hero voice that says, "I AM THE GREATEST," and, "I LOVE MYSELF." It is a mindset that even when we don't feel like progressing, we have hope and faith to keep moving forward because, "This too shall pass."

Make an action plan and remember "Repetition decreases Resistance." You must always expect to win. It's your mindset that creates all possibilities, so don't set your mind on negative, impossible, not me, or anything else that will get in your way and not allow God's work to enhance your being. Your only limitation is you.

There are three types of people in the world: Those who make things happen, those who watch things happen, and those that didn't even know something happened. Your mindset is crucial to Self-Love and Self-Love is crucial to a strong mindset.

I want you right now to remind yourself that you're amazing, you're a winner, and you have accomplished thousands of things in your magnificent life! We all too often think about our failures or mistakes, but listen to me my friend, please always remember that failure is an event, not a person. Failure should just be that, looked as an experiment that you learned from. Focus on the small things each day, correct those and get better 1% every day, and you will succeed. So, turn that Mindset around right now! Don't set your mind on the wrong things.

If you want to change directions in life, you have that choice. Sometimes, you will have to interrupt your old way of thinking by transforming your vocabulary, your attitude, and your beliefs, one day and 1% at a time. If I really want change, it's like turning on the light switch. I can flip the switch and bam, it is on, a change occurred. It is the time it takes to get to the light switch or the amount of time it takes us to make the change that matters most. It is the time it takes you to decide to make that change that takes the longest.

How much pain are you causing yourself and others by staying where you are in life? Let's move from pain to pleasure today. Starting today, find clarity of where you are now and where you want to be in life. Identify your strengths and talents that God gave you, and make a Plan of Action for the future. Decide to eliminate self-criticism and start giving yourself some self-compassion. Concentrate on your attributes, not your faults.

It might seem really hard at first but you can do it! I believe in you and I know your best days are yet to come. Starting today, you are now a glass half full kind of person, you will find a silver lining in all situations. Never forget your Attitude, not your Aptitude, determines your Altitude. GO BIG!

Plan-Prepare-Expect to win. Believe in yourself today. When you change your mindset, you change your story. When you change your story, you change your life. The journey of a thousand miles starts with a single step. A big part of your mindset is how you value yourself. So, what is Self-Esteem? Self-Esteem is confidence in one's own worth or abilities. Your Self-Worth, feeling of worthiness, confidence, self-respect, are all one. How do you see yourself? What is your personal value? Why is Self-Esteem important? Do you love yourself?

Two keys to Self-Esteem, are confidence and self-respect. You have to start out with loving yourself by building your Self-Esteem. Five ways to build Self-Esteem are:

> Use positive daily affirmations and staying intentional with your thoughts

> ➤ Identify your skillsets and then develop them
> ➤ Accept compliments
> ➤ Eliminate self-criticisms
> ➤ Affirm your real worth

We may have to experience a little pain sometimes before we can grow. Our brain tells us 100% of the time, to move away from pain and move to pleasure. As you transform, the pain is greater in the beginning, but in no time, a new habit is created and you begin to feel pleasure. You must STOP the recording of bad news and pain, then START the new recordings of how great and wonderfully made you are.

I can't complete this chapter without making sure you know that it is impossible to change a mind that is set. If you have a mind set to not change, then you will not change. So right now, change your mindset by using mind over matter, and faith over fear. My question to all of my champions that are reading this is, "What can you change today in your life, or give up, to start living the life you've always dreamed of?"

Change your attitude. Change your environment. Get out of your comfort zone and you will find your true passion, your zone of genius. Take one hour for yourself every day for spiritual and mental growth. Every day, you take a bath to wash the stink off of you and such is the same every day for your mindset. I need Jesus and motivation in me every day to help me achieve my goals and maximize my level of my ability. When we inspire, influence, impart, and introduce new habits and work on our Mindset daily, we begin to transform our lives. The secret of your success is determined by your daily agenda. Positive decisions and discipline equal success. Good decisions today will give you a better tomorrow.

It is when you begin to tell yourself, "I am going to believe my dreams and my imagination and I know with perseverance, faith, determination, and hard work that I will succeed." You have succeeded in the past with these skills. When we have troubles in life, many times it was because you had put God on the side and tried to drive your own car. LET GO & LET GOD. When you have the right thinking, the right priorities, and the right perspective, you will succeed.

Use your strength as fuel every day. Find things that make you feel empowered. Find positive people to surround yourself, events, videos, podcasts, and messages that keep you moving forward. Anyone or anything that doesn't move you forward or stronger, then it needs to be dumped. Turn your pain into purpose. Remember, progress equals happiness. Going forward, constantly progressing keeps us happy in life.

When we make the right choices, not because they are popular, but because they are right, we begin to show others how to manage life's ups and downs. For it is not failure in life that happens to us that develops our character; it is how we handle and deal with the trials and tribulations that show our true character. What do you need to do today to bridge the gap between your current situation, and your life as you've always dreamed about? You're born to succeed. You are born for success.

What is success? Who defines it? I define it as impacting others, creating value in others, inspiring others, influencing others, and imparting wisdom. We want to have a stronger mindset and we want to choose to win. That starts with expecting the best, preparing for the worst, and capitalizing on what comes.

Here are three things to focus on moving forward:
- What you have
- What you can control
- The present and future goals

We are all magnets; we are either chargers or drainers ourselves. We need to surround ourselves with battery chargers. Who you surround yourself with truly matters. Here are five things to do today to change your life:
- Feed and strengthen your mind
- Feed and strengthen your body
- Find a role model/mentor
- Find a plan and create action
- Find someone worse off than you and help them

Let's talk about goals. Without goals, we have no direction. Once I have goals, I have a map, my purpose. You need to set short-term, mid-range, and long-term goals. 97% of people never set goals. Be that ordinary person who ends up doing extraordinary things. People like Mother Theresa and Ghandi were simply ordinary people who did extraordinary things in their lives. Your dream life starts now with your powerful mindset and setting goals. When you're writing down your goals, you need to think: What is my passion and how can that passion serve others? Where do I see my life? You need to visualize what your dream life looks like.

Ask yourself, very specifically, what you want in your life. Then you want to ask yourself, how do I attain my goal? Is my goal realistic? Lastly, what is the timeframe of this goal? One day, one month, one year, or 5, 10, 20, 30 years down the road?

You have to see it to believe it. It is only a dream until you write it down and then it becomes a goal. Again, 97% of people never set goals! Where do you want to go in life? Do you know that you have choices and that you can make a choice? Who do you want to be? What kind of house do you want to live in, car do you want to drive, lifestyle, charity do you want to impact? How will you get there? It starts with goals, vision boards, and writing it down.

There are seven steps to setting a goal:
- Identify the goal
- List the benefits, what is in it for me?
- List the obstacles that you have to overcome
- List the skills and knowledge that's going to be required
- Identify people or groups to work with to accomplish this goal
- Develop a plan of action
- Develop a deadline for achievement of this goal

Never limit your goals, and never put a ceiling on your excellence. Life is a Journey not a Destination. I was visionpassionate about God, Family, and Friends. It is passion that makes the difference, for when we have passion, we have a love for something. Make a choice from today forward to live life with a passionate heart.

All the things that you want in life can be accomplished with massive action and overcoming fear. When you feel like you have something deeper and bigger inside of you, use your talent to move that feeling to the next level. When someone doesn't know what the next step is, but they know what they want to change, they say, "What is next?" This is where you can help someone else. Start by asking questions. If this was the last day of my life, what would I do? What would I say? Who would I talk to? Let's live our lives to the fullest. We have to live life full, otherwise it will live us. Stop and smell the roses. Appreciate being alive.

Remember, quitting is a permanent solution to a temporary problem. Always look to the future with joy in your heart and you will make your place in the world. Do you decide to get up each and every day and be the person you want to be? Yesterday really did end when you went to bed. You begin a new day each day when you wake up. Each day is what you make it. When the alarm goes off, do your feet hit the floor? Do you take a cold shower and jump in and hit the ground running? Or do you hit the snooze button eight times? Remember, you can have everything you want in life if you just help enough others get what they want and need.

Become a person of influence. Use insights to make a difference. You need to find out what others need and then serve them. We are in the service industry. Inspire someone today that needs a kind and supportive loving word, for your word may be the only one that they get. True joy comes from helping others on a path that most benefits him or her. Overthinking is the art of creating problems that don't exist. Don't do it. You can't change the beginning of the story, but you could certainly change the end of it. Remember, an idle mind operates in the devil's playground. Live and answer the call of what you were meant to do, and it starts with finding your purpose and passion in life. Think outside the box. Have a plan of action and a call to action. People will hurt you sometimes, and they will try to pull you back. They will pull you back to their comfort zones. You have to move forward and progress in life.

So, what can you do today to start that mental attitude of a warrior? Expect some pain on your path to growth. Tomorrow is never a given. What do you need to do today to take massive action? Each and every day when we wake up, we should be thankful. We should be inspired. We should be inspired for yourself and for others. Smile. Live life; it's short. Be happy. Remember now more than ever, we need to get back to the basics; faith, hope, and love. The greatest of all is love. We need to love more, to God, to family, and to friends.

Here are 10 behaviors to give up today:
- ➢ Excuses
- ➢ Self-Doubt
- ➢ Fear of failure

- ➢ Procrastination
- ➢ People pleasing
- ➢ Fear of success
- ➢ Negative thinking
- ➢ Negative self-talk
- ➢ Judgment of yourself and others
- ➢ Negative people in your circles

Remember the story about the Caterpillar? Just when he thought the world was over, he became a butterfly. What will be your transformation spiritually, mentally, and physically? Will you be strong, brave, and courageous? Will you train your mind to see the good in every situation? Remember, life starts with Self-Value, relationships, motivation, passion, and inspiration to name a few. Plato once said, "Remember this, no human condition is ever permanent. If you remember this, you will not be overjoyed in good fortune nor too scornful in misfortunes."

Trust in God, his plans are bigger than the ones you have for yourself. Each day, wake up and say, "I can do this. I am thankful. I have hope. I am confident in my abilities, because I am a champion!" I know my time is limited, so I can't waste it living someone else's life. I have to live my best life today. Life is too short to be anything but happy. Lack of direction not lack of time is the problem. You have 24 hours a day, 168 hours a week, 1,440 minutes a day. What are you wasting your minutes doing?

Your success isn't built on what you have. Your net worth doesn't determine your Self-Worth. It is built on your significance and your legacy. Your legacy is what you leave inside of others. Inheritance is what you leave behind, like money, property, etc. Each day, praise God and be thankful for God, family, and friends that you have in your life. It's very important to have great relationships with them.

<u>BIO</u>

Michael Merritt is an Inspirational Speaker, Author, Life Coach, Podcaster, Founder of Merritt Coaching Group, and Michael has been an EMT/ Firefighter since 1994. He is the Owner and Instructor for Advanced Medical Training. He started his career in the fire service and employed with Sherman Fire Department for over 10 years. On his days off, Michael taught American Heart Advanced Adult and Pediatric Life Support Certification classes. He worked as a Paramedic for various emergency departments, ambulance services, and event companies. In 2010, he moved to a quality position at Methodist Charlton and became the Quality Coordinator for the Cardiac Cath Lab. He has taught American Heart Association Certification classes for over 20 years. His motto is, "Saving Lives Through Education."

Website: http://merrittcoachinggroup.com
LinkedIn: http://linkedin.com/in/michael-w-merritt-90909447
Facebook: https://www.facebook.com/motivationinspirationknowledgebroker/
Instagram @michaelmerrittspeaking

10

Jason Floyd: *By The Grace Of God, Go I*

At seventeen I graduated high school. I think I was ready for my next chapter, ready to be out of the house and to get on with adulthood. I felt that going into the military would help me with that. My brother Brian had gone into the Army before me and I knew that was also going to be the path I took. Looking back on it, Brian showed me a way out. Even though David was a good guy, he wasn't my dad. My dad was never in my life and still isn't. As a young man, the Army offered more than just a way out of Van Buren, Arkansas. It offered adventure, stability, structure and dominant role models. All of which had been sorely lacking in my life. Plus, I truly wanted to serve my country.

My oldest brother Brian had been a Cavalry Scout. I followed him in with only that thought in mind. 19Delta could be and would be the only MOS for me. First, to a 17-year-old kid the designation 19Delta sounded "badass" and so did the description of a Cavalry Scout. Never regretted that decision. In MEPS I took the ASVAB, but never asked what I qualified for. When I walked in to talk about that I said I only wanted 19Delta and my MOS became 19D. I loved my job even in the bitter cold of the Kosovo Mountains or the uber hostile territories of Iraq. I wanted to be and sometimes needed to be 19Delta. It defined my twenties. 19Delta gave me purpose and Self-Worth and provided a level of responsibility I craved. Hell, we worked with Air Force TacP specialists and called in airstrikes! Now, it was training and the strikes were dummies, but it was some of the coolest training I have been through.

At seventeen years old I went off to basic training and AIT at Fort Knox, Kentucky. Away from home for the first time in my life and for sixteen weeks. Basic and AIT were combined so I did not go home in between the two. After eight weeks we were granted a weekend so Brian came up for the weekend and we hit the town. I was still only seventeen, but we enjoyed some beers just the same. When

I graduated after sixteen weeks my mother and David came up for the ceremony. I knew my first post was Germany and that I would get two weeks leave before heading out. I went home and did as close to nothing as a human could do. I sat around the house, drank beer and little else. Caught a commercial flight out of Fort smith, Arkansas bound for Atlanta. From there it was on to Germany and the start of my life as 19Delta. That was a long flight to say the least. Oddly, upon arriving in Germany I found that my recruiter had returned to his unit and was now stationed at Baumholder as well. I already knew someone!

Baumholder Army Base or United States Army Garrison (USAG) is affectionately nicknamed "The Rock" is located in the Rheinland of western Germany. Upon our arrival to "The Rock" we were immediately placed in a holding unit till our regular units could claim us. So here we are "wet behind the ears" PFC's and a sergeant from your unit comes to get you. His job is to "smoke" you all the way back to your unit. What do I mean by "smoked"? With all your gear on you are doing pushups, sit-ups and run till every ounce of energy has left your body. Then you will run some more for good measure. Throw in whatever sadistic plan that sergeant can dream up in his head and that is being "smoked". You arrive at your unit unable to fully function, which is just the way everyone else arrived. It was awesome!

This is where 19Delta got in my blood. It's where I became an important part of a team, where my Self-Worth got its biggest boost. As a Cavalry Scout my job was to be out, miles ahead of the main force. I, along with others in my unit, take positions above the enemy force and in real time report our observations. Troop movements, how fortified they are and their available fire power. Our accuracy saves or costs lives, American lives, and allied forces' lives. Those reports determine we may or may not attack an enemy force. Our teams usually consisted of 4 to 6. There was a Section leader (E6), Squad Leader (E5) and two to four scouts. From 1999 to 2001 I honed my skills as a Cavalry Scout in the mountains of Western Germany and in the mountains of Kosovo. Pretty cool for a country boy from Arkansas.

During that time, we went to live in Kosovo. The war there was winding down and we were sent in, along with allied forces, for peace keeping missions. There were band of Albanians, Macedonians and Yugoslavians that weren't satisfied and were still looking to fight. Even though Kosovo wasn't considered a "hotspot" anymore it was good for us because we worked with other nations of NATO to keep the peace and gather intelligence. We worked check points and observation points throughout the country. In particular, we worked with Russian forces on OP's (observation points). I remember we had strict orders for light and sound discipline. That means when it was zero degrees Fahrenheit, we could have zero fires for heat. We had to cover up any light source used for any reason while in use. Use was at a minimum. No sound, which meant radio silence. No one lit a match they could cover and if you smoked you did that in silence and his glow of the cherry red end. We were observing a local town. On the next hill the Russian troops were playing music, had huge bonfires and were keeping themselves warm with vodka! So much for discipline. We wanted to be there partying with them though. We were freezing. Our gun barrels were freezing so to combat that we had to use the liquid from our MRE warmers. We kept our food between our legs or down by our feet in the sleeping bag to keep it from freezing. By the way while we were eating MRE popsicles the Russians were roasting chickens on their bonfires and washing it down with vodka. Good times.

In my time in the military that time spent in Kosovo was also the worst for hiking. We would have an OP that we needed to get to up at the top of a mountain. The route might be three miles, but because of the rugged terrain, vertical assent and obstacles it felt every bit of fifty miles. Then we would get to the OP only to find our line of sight to obscure. We would pack up and move to the next mountain top. Of course, that also meant higher elevations. Thinner air and colder temperatures. At that age the physical part doesn't bother you too much, looking back it makes shake my head. A part of me will always miss even the most miserable parts. I definitely loved what I did and the cold and harsh conditions in Kosovo were just part of it. When I arrived in Germany, I was a "wet behind the ears" PFC, but when I returned home, I was a highly skilled Sergeant (E5).

Back home I landed at Fort Polk, Louisiana. When I got settled, I was assigned to the HQ unit. It really irritated me. While other guys with my skillset were being assigned to Ghost Troop, Delta Troop or Echo, I was stuck in S1 or S2. I sat in on all troop movement, all discussions on how we would deploy and what went into the decision-making process. I wanted to be in the field though. That's what I trained for. It slowly began to damn on me though, whenever the different troops were out in the field freezing and miserable, I was sleeping in my warm bed. Also, I realized I was learning how valuable my MOS 19delta really was. I got to see firsthand how that information was disseminated and acted upon. It gave me a new perspective. I spent six months in situation rooms honing the mental part of my game. HQ is a big part of my story and the demons because it's where I met one of my best friends and brothers. That man still haunts me today.

After six months in HQ, I was assigned into Ghost troop. Captain Brian Mescall who became a very good friend and brothers was assigned as our commander. I was now a squad Leader. We trained with Air Force TacP or Tactical Air Control Party Specialist, as I mentioned before, and learned all about calling in air strikes, which may be one of the coolest jobs in the military. As the pilot makes his run, he is communicating in real time with the TacP. The TacP might have the pilot run a string of telephone poles to line up a target and the pilot is all too happy to do it just before he drops a smart bomb into a gopher hole from 5000 feet. In January 2003, Ghost Troop was in gunnery when top brass visited us. Ghost Troop was informed that we were headed for Iraq. We were going to war. No more games, no more practice or training. It was time to "buck up"! We were told we were the perfect unit for this Iraq, our collective thought "Fuck Yeah!"

Two weeks later, we were on a C-17 with all our equipment, vehicles and gear headed for Kuwait. As soon as we landed, we were greeted by alarms going off all over the city. We had to put on our Mop Suits before departing the plane. Saddam's chemical warfare plans in full effect.

Missile strikes were also happening in and around the city so we were flown to an undisclosed location. As we got off the plane, we thought this undisclosed location was right in the middle of this chaos. It was 2003 and I was seeing the world. We spent two weeks in Kuwait before heading out for Iraq. The main force moved in a straight line toward Baghdad and we had mop up duty.

If they were the broad strokes, we were the fines lines. As they barreled through Iraq toward a meeting with Saddam Hussein, we made sure their flank was secure. We closed up any open wound that might fester in their wake. We cleared every town, every bridge and every dispute between Kuwait border and Sadr City. As soon as we crossed the Iraqi border, we were greeted with three loud booms and thought "Hell yes, it's on!" In reality, one of our own had a misfire with a Mark 19 grenade launcher hitting a building and destroying it. We then got the "come to Jesus" speech and were told to get our shit together as I recall. That is how Iraq started for me. The time I spent in Iraq was violent. We were assigned to Sadr City, nicknamed "Saddam City" because it was the most violent place in Iraq. It was where all the criminals were. We nicknamed our base of operations Camp Marlboro because it had been a cigarette factory in better times. We stayed there from April of 2003 to June 2004. Some of those ghosts that haunt me now died during that very violent time. War is brutal and war with an enemy that believes that God wants them to die while killing you is next level brutal. We lost Cpl. Sotello first. Right out of the gate, he lost his life to an IED. He was my roommate's best friend. Our Major lost his arm to the same IED.

Muqtada al Sadr ordered a hit on us and Eagle Troop was ambushed. Sgt. Swisher died there. Private Silva, who was in country less than two weeks was shot and killed. Eagle Troop was hit again and Sgt Tannish, a very close friend, was hit in the neck with shrapnel. He kept firing his weapon until he ran out of ammo, and then died. I can see them all. Sgt. Tannish and I used to go fishing together all the time at Fort Polk. His father was the Sgt. Major at Polk at one time. This was not statistics or stories we heard, these men were our brothers, our friends. This went on for fifteen months, but those first brothers are the ones I see, the ones that keep me awake at night. My mind never stops thinking about them. It never stops asking me "what if?" Captain Mescall haunts me most though, for different reasons.

In June of 2004, I went home to Fort Polk. In November of that year became an E6 Staff Sgt. As a Staff Sgt. I received orders for Fort Drum, New York. Fort Drum was on the Northern border of New York State. It is the home of the famous 10th Mountain Division. Before leaving Fort Polk my friend and former Commander Captain Mescall (who would become Major) asked me to go back to Germany with him. I turned him down because I felt I had already done my time in that region. We parted friends and went our separate ways. He to Germany and eventually Afghanistan and me to Fort Drum where I would be discharged from when my tour of duty was up. Before leaving for Fort Drum, I had 30 days leave. I went home to Western Arkansas where, again, I did less than nothing, but this time I had earned that right. I spent the last six to nine months of my enlistment there and by late 2005 I was a civilian again. After six years I did not re-enlist, but instead headed back to Van Buren, Arkansas. Things quickly went downhill from there.

November 2005, I arrived home and immediately started to drink. Since I had nothing to do but think, I drank to forget. The more I thought the more I drank. I became a functioning alcoholic. I went from structure, violence, training and Self-Worth to a void that I filled with bad memories, "what ifs" and alcohol. Many days I did not even eat. Just woke up and drank. Like a bad movie going off in my head, I would quell the demons with booze. It was 2006, when I decided to put a gun to my head in Natural Dam, Arkansas. Something had to change. I contemplated going back to the Army, but by that time I had replaced self-worth with self-loathing and I simply could not see the Army taking me back.

I had a plan. I would go off deep into the woods. I knew the place and I knew that it would be quite a while before anyone found me. In my mind no one understood me or what I was going through. No one cared and I did not want pity. I knew this was not going to stop unless I stopped it. I jumped on my ATV and headed out to complete my mission. About half way to my destination, I ran out of gas. I turned the fuel level to reserve and got the ATV back on the road. I knew this was a one-way trip and I would not need any more fuel to get me home. I only made it a half mile further though before I was completely out of fuel. I could not even do this right! An older couple came upon me and offered to help. Odd thing about getting help when you need it and least expect it, hope creeps in. I did not realize right then, but that small act of kindness saved my life. I would have completed my mission, but God had other plans. By his grace, I am here today.

I met my wife later that year and went to work at the last job I would ever have. Baldor is the same company my mother worked for. I started to get on with my life. The demons were still there, but I had something filling the gap. I reached out to now Major Mescall via email to ask about what ribbons and medals we earned in Iraq. I did not hear back from him so I reached out again, but to no avail. One day I was corresponding with another of my brothers from Ghost Troop when he asked me if I had heard about "Capt. Mescall" (we always knew him as such)? I said no and he drop the worst possible news on me. Our commander from Ghost Troop and my friend had been killed in action. Capt. Mescall died by IED along with everyone else in the vehicle. Would I have been in that vehicle? All the Self-Worth that I had built in training on mountaintops in Germany and Kosovo and battle hardened in Iraq came into question just as it did when I returned home. Except this time, it was much worse.

Capt. Mescall wanted me on his team and I denied his request. I should have been there. If I had gone, could I have saved him or anyone else? The answer is no, I would have died like everyone else, but even to this day that demon haunts my irrational thoughts. The unanswered questions erode my rational mind and expose raw feelings. They deny me sleep. They deny me peace at times and make me question whom I am and if any of the good I may have done, was really worth me continuing to be here. For someone rational and without demons of doubt this may seem ridiculous, but we who suffer know it is very real. Brian passed in 2009. While we were not that close, I still see him as my closest relative. He knew what it meant to take an oath and say you will die for your country. There are those lost in Iraq and My good friend in Afghanistan. Each one intensifies the self-loathing and doubt. These demons chase me and like in any dream, I simply cannot run fast enough to get away.

My wife is a strong and loving woman. Through her I find strength, my faith in God has not waivered through my life. Some would say I should get a pass on God because of all I have been through in my life. I would submit to those people that because of that faith I have survived. Especially before my wife came to me. I was going to take my life, but by his grace, an old couple gave me hope. I do not think that I have been saved while others die or that God chooses one child over another. I think that we are humans with free will and that Nature's God has set the wheels in motion to allow nature to take its course. Sometimes in the course of that nature, we are helped and sometimes it comes too late, but for the grace of God, go I. The answers beyond that are above my pay grade. I know that at my lowest points I saw signs that saved me and I wish others could see those signs. My faith in god is still strong and gets stronger every day.

One day I decided, as I was driving home from work, that I wanted to know more about the Masons. My grandfather was a Mason and I had heard so many good and bad things about them that I simply needed to ask. The sign outside the Lodge said, "Ask 1 to be 1" so I showed up on a Lodge night and did just that. A very nice older man name David told me a little (very little) about the Lodge and handed me a petition. I petitioned the Lodge and was accepted, but not before three Masons met me at the Lodge to question my intentions. The first question was "Do you believe in God?" I answered yes and moved forward. Had I said no our conversation would have ended and they would have said good night? See you cannot be a Mason if you do not believe in God. It is deeper than that though. Everything in Masonry is focus around the Grand Architect of the Universe. That was so important to me. It is very important to them as well. We take an oath to God. It is not a secret. You can go on the internet and read all about it. Most of what you read is pure fiction, but the wackos do not mind. People believe in ignorance rather than the truth. Just look at our government.

Becoming a Mason has helped my ability to cope daily. I do not identify with most people. I do not believe they understand why my oath means so much to me. My wife is an exception because she always there to pick up the pieces. That oath I took as a Mason helped me because they believe in their obligations to God and each other. While being around people is always a struggle, the mere fact that my Mason brothers identify with me and my oath gives me that strength one can only receive in numbers. The sweetest part is we do everything for God. Before I became a Mason, I got on the internet and found that the hatred for all things Masonic was based solely in ignorance and jealousy. I could not substantiate anything I read. None had been Masons. Most parroted what other conspiracy theorists were saying. What I knew was I am my own man and I would find out for myself. It has been an amazing experience. Covid tested every new Mason. We had to comply with laws and it set many of us back. Those of us who have been patient are moving forward becoming better men and better citizens, but most of all stronger in our conviction to God and each other.

As I mentioned previously I do not like being around people. I worked for only one company since leaving the Army. Only two employers since I became an adult. During the Covid year of 2020, I had a down turn. Masonic Lodges were dark meaning we could not attend because of Covid. I would go to work each day and my thoughts became dark. I felt like, in the right situation, I might hurt someone. My condition seem to be getting worse. I could not sleep because the one thing that keeps me going had eroded. For me it is my Self-Worth. I measure my overall health and well-being by my Self-Worth. It may be a byproduct of the environment I grew up in, but for whatever reason it is what drives me and what kills me. I have been seeing Psychologists and Psychiatrists for years and they have really helped me. Therefore, when I went to them and said I am afraid I may hurt someone if I continued to work, they listened. They ramped up the evaluations and medications and eventually they put me on 100% disability. I fought that for years simply because I did not want to live off the government. I talked to friends I trusted enough to confide in and talked to my wife (who was the biggest influence) and asked for help. My self-worth came into play here, but I had to realize that I could not work on a better version of me if I even contemplated hurting other for a minute. 2020 was a tough year of medication changes and deep depression and recovery if you can call it that. I take one day at a time.

I have no children. I have animals that act like children. In 2020, I added 4 alpacas, Spitfire, Q-Tip, Tina and Bob. Six goats, including Fugly who thinks he is a dog and wonders the property eating dogfood and always wanting attention. Ram, Bam Fully, Lil Girl, Hank and Rita round out the goat herd. Our miniature horse is Drama Queen and the turkey are Harry, Lloyd, Bert and Ernie. There is also numerous dogs, duck and chickens. It is therapy to be out among them. Feeding and caring for them helps me. It has its difficulties. When I got the alpacas home, I knew they spit. The first time I experienced that I was not prepared for quart or so that washed over me! I have a favorite dog; Dixie is an old pug who is a constant companion. I do not think people realize how much those animals help their owners. There is good reason for therapy dogs. Animals do not judge you; they do not care about your success or your failures. They care about eating! They care about attention. Bob the alpaca cares about being left alone and Dixie the pug can sense my moods and is always there. No matter what though all of them rely on me to be there for them and it gives me a sense of purpose. Working my property or helping an older neighbor in need these things are therapy for me. You have to find a purpose. There has to be reasons to get up in the morning. Through it, all stands my loving wife. She does not deny me my many therapies. She always supports me through thick and thin. That more than all else combined drives me to carry on and do better. She works in physical therapy and by her very nature knows how to nurture. She is patient and kind to me. That patience, which I am sure she shows her patience, has helped me through many battles. Still the demons come, but it is getting better. I have surrounded myself with only those people that I feel care enough about me to contribute to my health and well-being by their very presence. I do not ask anything of them and am grateful for their friendship. I am uncomfortable receiving gifts, but love giving them. I am becoming a better man and Mason every day as well. Through the love of my wife, loyalty of my animals and the brotherhood of the Masons I walk through this place gaining that worth that so often eludes me. Part of that is because none of those mentioned above judge me. They only ask how they can help.

I have learned that you have to know what you mean to others. I never learned that as a child. There was no role model for me. You have to find something to live for and something to fight for. I found that in my wife. You have to have those in your life that simply do not judge, but accept your flaws, warts, and are not afraid to show you their own. I found that in the Masons and realized that we are a lot alike in that we can just take those things we need to work on and look to the next brother who already has his hand out willing to help. My experience is needed there. They want me to grow and mentor others. It drives me to have goals and to achieve those goals with my brothers.

Unfortunately, my story is not unique. Many of my comrades have come home to find themselves lost. We lose too many brothers and sisters every day to these horrors of war, these demons that drag us into a belief that we are not worth anything here at home. Nothing could be farther from the truth. It is hard for me to hear someone say I am a hero.

I am not, but I do understand those who believe that those who served should be considered heroes because I think others who served or are serving are heroes. If you are suffering, please ask for help and keep fighting the good fight. I mean this when I say it; By the Grace of God go I, but also you. Many of our brothers and sisters did not coming home the way their families had hoped and many did not come home at all. Some of us who did feel guilty about that or wished we hadn't, but you are needed and your worth is important and if you need help get it and maybe someday your story will help another lost soul get home.

<u>BIO</u>

Jason Floyd is 100% medically retired 19D from the US Army. He struggles every day with PTSD but is working on his demons. He lives in Booneville, Arkansas with his wife and many animals that helps him cope with mental health conditions developed from war. He is also a Masonic Mason which has helped him more than the therapist, psychiatrist and pills. Jason has decided to step into a new mission to help others with low Self-Esteem find their new mission after life has knocked them down.

11

Tamara Patzer: *To Say That 2020 Was Surreal Is An Understatement*

To say that 2020 was surreal is an understatement. As millions of us hunkered down, life continued. My granddaughter Olivia was born on 4/29/2020 at 4:28 p.m., so who knows what that magical moment means for her. Olivia is the best thing that has happened to this grandmother in the past year. Olivia has been my rock, my foundation, and my hope.

As a lifelong introvert, my goal in life has always been to be invisible. At age 4, I hid behind my father's knee and peered out at the world or the huge humans who would bend down and pinch my cheek. I didn't like it. Even my grandmother would pinch my fat cheek and say, "My little Tami!" and I didn't like it.

Baby Olivia has been the joy and highlight of my life, and I look at her and admire how she approaches her world and me. When Olivia's daddy carries her into the room to see me, she immediately squeals and smiles at me with the acknowledgment that she *sees* me and loves me. I, in turn, squeal and feels waves of delight as she reaches out to me and buries her little head into my neck and snuggles. This is the essence of being in the NOW.

Being a grandmother is similar to being the guardian of your business. Like a new baby, your business is fresh and innocent when born and grows via milestones. Like a baby who sleeps most of the day as it grows internally, a business needs constant care and feeding and moments of silence as it develops and matures.

My business is nearly 11 years old now, a pre-teenager, but as I look at Olivia, who just turned the magic 1-year-old, I can see the lessons I have learned as I grew as the guardian of my business and became more visible. With that, I want to share some lessons that you can apply to recognize your own zone of genius as you go from being invisible to become a credible authority expert.

Be Authentic and Real

Olivia laughs when she is happy. She cries when she is hungry or wet. Olivia squeals with delight when she sees her grandmother or the kitty. She is real and in the moment.

Think about it? Do you live your life with templates, scripts, and rehearsals? Is every moment perfect? No.

After many failed starts at becoming an Entrepreneur, I finally beat "JOB" addiction and started my business in 2009. I earned my Master's degree in Mass Communications and Instructional Technology.

My first online adventure was "Main Street Marketing Machines" with Mike Koenigs. I was working full-time for Help-U-Sell Real Estate in Sarasota, Florida, and it was a long two-hour commute, each way, five days a week, for about $17 an hour. I was tired and under-appreciated, so I invested the famous $1997.00 paid in payments of $587.00 every month. I knew I had to make a least $587 a month to make it pay for itself. The trouble with Main Street Marketing Machines was that, in reality, it didn't have the training I needed to move from being an employee to an Entrepreneur. Still, luckily one of the bonuses from Jim Cockrum was exactly what I needed to move from the real world of the JOB to becoming a Marketing Consultant. Within six months, I was truly self-employed, and I said to good-bye to the JOB and the commute.

As I have been outlining these lessons from Olivia about becoming visible, the word FEAR jumped out at me.

Many of you, especially women, say, "Oh, my God, I have to put on makeup. I have to do something with my hair. I have to wear certain clothes. I have to do this, that and the other thing." With all these woes and worries, guess what doesn't happen? You end up not making videos that will help you grow your business. *Olivia doesn't worry about how she looks!*

Live video showing you works well, as I explained when I talked about my plastic surgeon client. But the truth is you, don't need to show your face on video, but it is better if you do. I hear you now, complaining about the sound of your voice.

Olivia doesn't worry about the sound of her voice or the fact that she doesn't have many words. She talks and babbles and smiles.

Think about it. A baby doesn't worry about anything. They live in the moment and the now. You should take that advice!

You must get over the fear of being on video and talking on video. Get over all of these little details that stop you from becoming the successful person you already are — that prevent you from being visible and finding your zone of genius. You have to claim it. You have to eliminate the dirty word "fear" from your vocabulary. They say that fear is false evidence appearing real. We know that the things we are often afraid of aren't even real. Here's the reality, you look like you look. It doesn't matter if you are heavy or slim. Attractive, unattractive, we all are unique individuals. It just doesn't matter.

What are you afraid of? People are going to see you. Unless you live under a rock, right? Our voice is our voice. It's what makes us unique. Think about some of the most famous people and what their voices sounded like. John F. Kennedy comes to mine. Oprah. Phil, Dr. Phil, and his Texan accent. I have a friend who is from New Orleans, and he has a certain accent. Do not worry about what you look like or how you sound. Just be you.

Six Steps To Eliminate Fear

As I have been outlining these lessons from Olivia about becoming visible, I realized that she has given me six steps to take to eliminate fear of being visible, especially online and on video!

First, take a deep breath. Relax. Incorporate meditation, and meditation can be in your head or external. It doesn't have to be you sitting somewhere cross-legged saying, "Om"; it can be as simple as closing your eyes and taking a deep breath.

Breathe. Breathe in, breathe out, breathe in, breathe out.

When you breathe in and out, your mind and body will start to go into the rhythm of being relaxed so that you can tune out and turn up those fear thoughts.

Second, use visualization. See yourself successful. See the result of what happens when you put yourself out there. Visualize how strong you are, see the smile on your face. See the audience responding to you. Visualize the positive outcome.

Three, take baby steps. Take small steps. It will take time and a strategy to convince your subconscious that you're not afraid of whatever it is that is holding you back. Think about it; once you can face the fear of talking on video or being seen on video, it gets easier each time. Start with just doing a simple slide and talking and recording it. Write yourself a script; you don't need to, but it helps. Just do something to move forward.

Number four, do what you fear if you're scared to talk on video, talk. If you're afraid to appear on video, appear on the video. It's easy. You can use simple free tools like Zoom, Skype, or Facebook Live. There are many tools out there for you to use. Just do it.

Number five, build up your Self-Esteem. Use your small successes. Build upon them, and pretty soon you'll have one, two, three, four, and hundreds of videos, and you'll wonder, "Why didn't I start sooner?"

Number six, interrogate yourself. After you have identified and isolated your absolute worst fears, ask yourself a series of questions about them that are designed to help you understand more. What is the worst thing that can happen? What can I do to minimize my fear? Who's going to listen to me? Who's going to judge me? Why am I afraid to be judged by others about the way I look or how I sound? Is my message valuable to others? What if the knowledge that I possess can help somebody else have a better life? That's a really good question. Who are you not to share your message with the world?

Remember, fear was meant to help you survive from animal attacks, from somebody chasing you, from the dark because of the unknown. We don't live in a world where you have to be afraid of the dark anymore. We live in a world where you can use all of that energy to create a positive, impactful life for you and your family. So, ask yourself that question, "Who would ever listen to me?" Answer it honestly, and what you're going to find out is that a lot of people, many people, are hungry for your knowledge and they want to hear what you have to say.

Again quickly, use these six steps to manage your fear of being on video. Relax, use visualization, take small steps, do what you are afraid of, build up your Self-Esteem, ask yourself questions, and interrogate yourself about the worst thing that could happen if you start making videos.

The One-Minute Video Strategy

Video. Video. Video. Video is one of the best tools for any foot-in-the-door strategy, especially for local marketing consultants. Many scenarios encompass the use of video. One opportunity is local trade shows. Another is at local businesses or offices.

If you choose the trade show strategy, it might be advisable to check with the trade show promoters first. Ask them if you can record videos of their participants to help promote the trade show online. Most will oblige. If not, you can always walk around and ask the individuals at the booths. Try to find the principal or owner of the company to speak about their company for about a minute. *(Most representatives won't talk about the company if they don't have any authority or permission.)*

Of course, the idea with foot-in-the-door strategies is you're getting your foot in the door. In this particular strategy, with the video one-minute story, the idea is that you may meet them. It may be at their place of business, at a trade show, or a chamber of commerce event. It's an opportunity for you to say, "Hey, how about if I make you a little video where you're telling me about your business?"

Making a video is a really good icebreaker that you can use at a Chamber of Commerce networking event, club meeting, or community expo. It's easy. Arrive armed with your video camera, introduce yourself, and tell them a bit about your business. Then say, "Would you like a free video about your business?

They say, "Yes." You proceed with, "Tell me about your business." You could have a little pre-script made or explain what they need to say, which would be the five W's (Who, What, When, Where, and Why) plus How. For example, who are they? What is their business? What do they do? Where are they located? This probably will take about a minute or so.

Remember, you don't spend a lot of time on this video. You don't need to edit it. You can add a title, name tags, and possibly some content information. You can make each business a channel of their own on YouTube, or you could create your channel about your community where people could go to watch these one-minute community videos. Don't limit who you interview. It could be a nonprofit organization, a service organization, or it could be a business.

The idea is to get your foot in the door with a free video because it has great perceived value. If you are trying to think of a quick way to get attention from local businesses or any business for that matter, head out to an event and start using this easy strategy. The beauty of this strategy is that you can easily optimize the video to show off your video search engine optimization (SEO) skills.

Video + Email = Personal Introduction = Warm Lead

I have used video to become more visible since 2009. Even before that, I used to produce videos for real estate companies and had a TV show about real estate for sale in Southwest Florida called, Gulf Coast Property Review. While I was comfortable behind the camera, getting in front of it took courage and confidence.

As I became an Entrepreneur and was forced to become more extroverted, I relied heavily on videos to connect to potential clients. I learned about foot-in-the-door strategies from various local marketers, and I forced myself to use video. In 2009, my choices of video cameras were the famous Flip or Kodak Zi8. Today, you can use your cell phone. The quality of videos on iPhones and Androids is phenomenal, and you can use them to make your video productions. You can even use the "apps" on your phone to do editing. Now, you can also use Facebook Live or other methods, such as Zoom. They all work and can help you become visible.

The key to any effective foot-in-the-door strategy is to take action. Most of us have a major fear of public speaking and cold calling (one-to-one public speaking). How can you overcome this obstacle that can be one major roadblock in a successful sales career of any kind?

The Video Email Strategy is fun, easy, and powerful. Don't panic about the "how" for video emails. It's easy to make a video email. There are several ways to accomplish the creation of the video. A video can be created using a computer camera, an I-phone, or any video camera. Set up your camera to have your head and shoulders in the frame, and introduce yourself to the person you hope to meet or possibly met at a local networking event or function.

Tips For Video Email Success

- ➤ Write your script or talking points. Make it about 30 seconds to a 1-minute maximum.
- ➤ Introduce yourself. Use your name and a few sentences of what you do. End with a call to action. (Call me for details at 123-555-1212 or reply to this email)
- ➤ Don't try to sell anything.

Just say, "Hi, Name of Person, I'd thought you'd like to know about my services. My name is…" introduce yourself. What makes this so powerful is it is a strategy that you could say, "If you're interested in using this tool, I have many more that could help you get more customers and clients for your business."

Always show them the benefit of what you're doing that could help them. Again, video email introductions are very inexpensive. It takes a little time.

Before you record:
> Check your clothes, hair, etc.
> Just think of how you would dress and present yourself in person.
> Look as professional and confident as possible.

Video is a powerful foot-in-the-door strategy because it makes every call a warm call. Not only are you showing someone how unique and different you are by using this tool. You can use it as a tool that local businesses can use to get new clients and customers for themselves. It's the ideal tool to help create the "know, like, trust factor."

My favorite story about using this method is about my very first client. He was a local plastic surgeon with a beauty spa on the side. I found his website, and it was full of typographical errors, and I knew he needed me. I worked full-time, so I made a video early in the morning before work and sent it to him via email. He responded, and I got an appointment to see him. I told my boss I had a doctor's appointment, which was true. I wore the same outfit I had worn in my video, and when the plastic surgeon saw me, he hugged me. So, this told me that the power of video was just like being there. I discovered that video or today's Zoom calls are just as powerful as the "in-person" appointment!

Olivia has taught me a lot about being on video and making the camera work for her. As she has grown this past year, she recognizes the cell phone and turns on the charm with her energy as she looks into the camera and babbles and smiles. She instinctively knows how to put her positive energy into her video appearances.

She looks into the camera lenses as if she is seeing and talking to me, who is behind the camera. This is good advice to follow. So, be like Olivia and look into the camera and see the person you are talking to directly. It works, I promise.

Let's Go Out Or Stay In To Explore The World

As Olivia has grown over the past year, she is always ready to have a day out. She loves the outdoor adventures in the strollers and occasionally visits other local venues. Olivia's attitude about meeting other people in the world is: look, listen, and respond. If you think about it, this is a great strategy for getting new clients or customers. I call it the Let's Go Out! Strategy. *(You can use this strategy even in pandemic times. You have to tweak your definition of going out. Today, you might go out to a Zoom call, a ClubHouse audio call, webinar, or other online in-person events. My point is that you can use this in the physical world or virtual world.)*

While Olivia doesn't have the mobility to choose to go out into the world without help from Mom or Dad, often, adults, especially introverts, get what I call "stuck-butt syndrome."

Covid-19 was a slap in the face for many people, and they were trapped in their own homes. For introverts, like me, it was more of business as usual. It is easy to hide behind your computer and be invisible.

Ask yourself, "Do I have stuck-butt syndrome?" Do you hate to leave the comfort of the computer screen? Well, the reality is that even though "viral networking" is easy to do, "belly to belly" or "real world" networking will make you money faster — but, in pandemics, you do what you have to do.

Networking isn't cold calling. It's one proven way to get more business and certainly a way to move quickly to the "know, like, trust" factor in getting and doing business in the real world. The truth is we use online networking to move our potential clients and customers into the real world of doing business.

In this strategy, "Let's Go Out" means exactly that. Let's go out can mean you go out into the world via your feet or online connections. Let's go out to mix and mingle with people in their "real life" elements. Think about it. What do you like to do? Play golf? Play tennis? Hang out at networking events? Conventions? Trade shows? The message here is to get off the computer and go out into the world where your potential clients and customer live, work, and play. *(So, if you have hobbies but are stuck at home, you can still hang out with people online with the same interests. For example, you can join membership groups, online clubs, Facebook Groups, etc.)*

In the local world, chambers of commerce, referral groups, and community organizations rule. You don't need to become a member of any organization to benefit from them. Chambers of Commerce typically have non-members rates for any networking event. Business Networking International (BNI) groups often welcome guests a few times before they expect a commitment, and of course, clubs and organizations typically invite guests hoping to gain new members. *(Again, you can do all of these events online or offline!)*

Not only can you network at these events, but you can also offer to speak or deliver a presentation. Local groups are always looking for presentations that can be useful to their members. For example, local boards of Realtors look for presenters who can speak about social media, mobile marketing, or dos and don'ts about internet marketing and QR codes... think about what you KNOW, and most likely, you can develop a presentation about it. *(I use these examples because that's what I talk about, but you can talk about your expertise.)*

The "Let's Go Out" strategy can be simple to implement, but the key is IMPLEMENT. You have to take action and get off your duff to make this strategy work. Take action today. Just go online and find out what local events are happening today, tomorrow, or anytime this week and GO.

The beauty of it all is that you can go out even when you are inside your own home. You can become visible no matter where you are in the world!

Teach To Become Visible

Authority. Expert. Teacher. What do these three words have in common? If you can claim to be an authority, expert, or teacher, you have clout, and it will get your foot in the door in big ways.

There are many ways to show off your expertise and authority by teaching. For example, suppose you teach a workshop and show people how to use social media, make videos, create a Facebook page, a Twitter page, or a LinkedIn profile. In that case, people will come to your class, and either become your client or tell others what they learned from you!

One of the key reasons teaching works as an excellent foot-in-the-door strategy is that when people learn something, they will quickly figure out that it is not as easy as it appears. So, they often hire the "teacher" to get the work done for them.

Not sure how to set up a teaching event? There are many ways to do it. Here are three examples:

> Contact your local chamber of commerce and offer to do a free workshop
> Get in touch with your local extension service or community college and offer to do paid or free workshops
> Find a venue and set up your own paid or free workshops.

After sharing what baby Olivia has helped me learn in her first year of life, it reminds me that my journey as an introvert observer to authority, expert, teacher, and publisher has been a long one. It is obvious that we are born without embarrassment and have joy within us. Somewhere along the way, I learned to be afraid of showing my joy and laughter and had to stop and learn how to appear in front of other people on video and on television. I am grateful to Olivia for showing up in 2020 to help her grandmother understand the power of visibility.

<u>BIO</u>

Dr. Tamara "Tami" Patzer - creator and founder of the Daily Success® Institute, the home Quick Start, Fast Results business programs and courses, Women Innovators Publishing, Blue Ocean Authority, and Get Massive Media Exposure. Tami has a BA from Eckerd College in Creative Writing and Business, followed by a MA in Mass Communication and Instructional Technology from University of South Florida. An avid learner, Tami also received her Ph.D. in Metaphysical Science from Angel Ministries College in Venice, Florida. Her courses included in Daily Success® are all designed to include the latest and best in educational training for the ultimate learning experience with video, audios, workbooks, course books, action guides, check lists and step-by-step systems.

Website: https://www.dailysuccessinstitute.com
All social media platforms as Tamara Patzer

Sean Douglas: *You Were Made For Something Great!*

What was I created for? What is my purpose? I am sure that we have asked ourselves these very questions a time or two in our life. I am also sure that we have all been asked the infamous question by our parents or a school counselor; "What do you want to be when you grow up?' I wanted to be a farmer!

My grandparents lived in the country on a 10-acre farm. On weekends and in the summer, I would spend a lot of time with them there. We would ride horses, go fishing, cook out, and my favorite, plant vegetables in the garden and pick them when they were ready. I remember snapping the ends of peas from a big bowl and setting them aside to make string beans. I remember picking the harvest of corn, green beans, peppers, and other vegetables that we grew. I learned a lot from my time in the garden. How does something that tastes so good come from such a small seed? How does something so amazing grow in such a short amount of time?

I learned in the garden what it took to grow something of value, something of substance, and the joy of seeing what the hard work produced at the end of the growing season. It takes water, plant food, care, and love. In life, there are necessities that we require. In the same, we need food and water, but much more than that, we need care and love. Bullying has become its own pandemic in schools. During the Covid-19 pandemic, domestic violence rose, mental health issues increased, and the suicide rates skyrocketed. Without care and love, these conditions took center stage.

A Chinese bamboo tree takes five years to grow. It has to be watered and fertilized in the ground where it has been planted every day. It doesn't break through the ground for five years. After five years, once it breaks through the ground, it will grow 90 feet tall in five weeks! If you're feeling like your business isn't growing, your relationships aren't flourishing, or you feel stuck in life, just remember that the bamboo tree takes five years to grow, but once it does, it shoots up from the ground very quickly. Your relationships, your job, your business, even you, takes time to grow. Nothing is an overnight success. Many people who go to the gym will stare in the mirror after a workout wondering why it isn't working. Many Entrepreneurs will stare at their business financials wondering why they aren't making money. Many people will graduate high school or college wondering what's next in their life in hope that they made the right decisions to grow. What I will do here in the next couple pages is give you some practical steps for growth, because you were made for something great.

Childhood abuse can be an ugly reality for families. As a child that was abused, I would wonder what I did wrong. I would wonder why certain members of my family didn't love me. I would wonder if I should even stay in this world. When I went to school, I would be bullied. When I went home, I would be bullied. I walked around most of my childhood with my head down trying to stay out of people's way. I have always been an energetic person, but sometimes it felt like that was not what other people liked, and therefore, I tried to act a certain way around certain people to impress them. I tried to be the class clown so people would like me. I would say things or do things to gain acceptance, even though I may have regretted what I was doing at the time. When you act a certain way to impress someone else or to gain their acceptance, you begin the process of devaluing yourself.

I believe Acceptance is the most powerful and dangerous behavioral trait. A person's need to be accepted can make them do things or act a certain way that they normally would never do in other settings. Peer pressure can make a child smoke, drink, or perform an act that goes against how they were raised. The need to be accepted is more powerful than the threat of jail or harm. We all crave Acceptance, whether it be from our parents, from co-workers or peers, or from our spouses, or family. No one wakes up in the morning and asks to be hated. No one starts their day hoping that someone will bully them or make fun of them. It is the Acceptance that drives a person to act out of character, but where does the root of this behavior lie?

I always say that Core Values are the number one way that you will grow from no worth to Self-Worth. Your Self-Worth isn't determined by the clothes you wear because that's the style. Your Self-Worth doesn't increase because you acted how a certain group of people act. Your Self-Worth doesn't increase when you engage in behavior that tears down other people. Your value according to other people may increase because you are a hard worker, a great parent, a supportive spouse, or have become a person of value. That "brand value" is a matter of opinion and does not matter. What matters is how all that makes you feel. That is Self-Worth.

The vegetables in the garden did not change their value based on how I felt about them. The vegetable's value did not increase because I liked corn better than peas. The value of a certain vegetable was determined by me based on how much I liked them, which has nothing to do with the vegetable itself. So why do you try so hard to impress people who don't value you anyway? Why strive to impress someone else when you can strive to *grow* yourself? You cannot give from an empty cup no matter hard you try. Once you decide what your Core Values are, it is time to live by example. Once you begin to live out your Core Values, you begin to "Live Your Brand." There's a lot of talk online about branding and personal brand. Your personal brand is your Core Values, and you living out your Core Values, is you living your brand. I believe that is the difference between having no worth and having a strong sense of Self-Worth.

On an episode of my Podcast, Create Launch Monetize Podcast, my friend, Christopher Lochhead, Host of Follow Your Different and Lochhead On Marketing, said that brands are not people, and I agree. What you believe in is your brand. How you think, feel, and believe about yourself gives you brand value. That is what I believe is the next step after creating Core Values and living them. I remember the moment clearly when I found my brand value.

I suffered through child abuse, bullying, and negative thoughts and self-talk. I barely graduated high school thus cementing my future of never going to college. I was working at Discount Tire, living at home with my mom and sister, contemplating my future. Then, 9/11 happened. I thought to myself that this would be my dare to great moment. This moment in time would be the time that I decide my worth and I joined the U.S. Air Force. At the time, I thought that discipline and Core Values was what I needed, and I was right. What I didn't count on was a culture I was all too familiar with. The Military is a tough crowd and you will get eaten alive if you don't perform at an extremely high level. The culture within the confines of the Military

Industrial Complex can be a toxic one. I was thrust into a culture of, work hard, play hard. It was the norm after a 12-hour shift to hit the bars and drink away the day's problems. It was the culture to prank the new guys, belittle them, and show them tough love. You were constantly forced to prove your Self-Worth in a world where your life was in someone else's hands, and their life in yours. I guess that is to be expected. Everyone has a job to do and there is no time for mistakes. This enormous pressure for many 18–20-year-olds leads to drinking, or even depression. With extreme accountability, comes extreme behavior.

After developing a drinking habit, and mistakes I would make, I was facing the realization that maybe I didn't belong in the Military. I felt like a failure. I didn't feel accepted. This led to feeling worthless, which led to suicidal thoughts. Facing a possible administrative discharge, coupled with a failing marriage, the thoughts of suicide increased. Then the moment came. I told my mom what was happening and how my life was on a downward tail spin, and she gave me a book to read by Norman Vincent Peale, The Power of Positive Thinking. It was my first step towards personal development. I finished the book and started to realize that most of my behavior started with the need to belong. My behavior was rooted in how I thought people thought about me. I valued other people's opinions over how I thought about myself. I felt like I had no value, no worth, so why keep living? The realization came after putting into practice what I read, and talking with Military Chaplains. I was raised Roman Catholic but got away from God because I blamed Him for my life being in shambles. I decided that maybe I was more at fault than what I wanted to give credit to, and so I got to work.

I started reading personal development books and reading The Bible. I remember what the Priests had said at church about how I was fearfully and wonderfully made. I remember scripture after scripture about how we are blessed, how He loves us, and how prominent figures of The Bible were sinners, yet God used them for extraordinary moments. I started to identify with those great men of God like Saul who persecuted Christians but was then blinded on the road to Damascus. God calls Saul, Paul, for the first time, and he became the Author for most of what we know in the New Testament. Moses was a prince of Egypt, but also sometimes a coward and a murderer. Moses also was known to have a lack of confidence in speaking publicly. God called Moses to Midian in the form of a burning bush, and gave him Aaron so that he would fulfill God's purposes by freeing the people of Israel from the corrupt rule of Egypt and leading them to the promised land. Peter, once known as Simon, was a disciple who would become one of the earliest disciples of the church. Peter wasn't always bold, but he was always impulsive and often acted before thinking. Peter constantly questioned Jesus's teachings and his own faith, and even denied Jesus three times while being arrested. He would later become an anointed apostle of the church who did mighty miracles and preached powerfully in public. The story of David and Goliath is one of the most famous stories of The Bible, and is used in context many times. God used David to defeat the mighty Goliath who was bigger, stronger, and faster. How is all this possible?

Whether you believe in God, a higher power, or don't believe anything, something, or someone, created you. You were made for something great, and I believe everything happens for a reason.

A noticeable change was happening inside of me. I was developing a renewed outlook on my life. My Captain told me that I should apply to become an Air Force Basic Training Drill Instructor and to go back to my roots of discipline and Core Values. I was accepted, and my journey of developing my own Self-Worth was set in motion. For four years, I learned how to teach, train, speak, and develop confidence within myself and those entrusted to my charge. I learned how to coach and mentor young men and women who had also experienced a hard knock life. I had found my purpose. I had found my calling.

At the end of my four years as a Military Training Instructor, I was sent to a new duty station. I met a man who would be instrumental in the further development of my purpose. He asked me to come on as a Master Resilience Trainer teaching Mental, Physical, Social, and Spiritual Resilience skills to the military servicemen and women. It was here where I learned the power of Gratitude, to balance my own thinking and to think more positive, and to develop a Spiritual Resilience. Spiritual Resilience is defined as the ability to sustain an individual's sense of self and purpose through a set of beliefs, principles or values. I embodied this life change and put into practice every day to become a person of value, to myself, and to those around me, no matter what they thought about me. I learned to value my own self and my own opinions over the opinions of others. I was also given the opportunity to become the Suicide Awareness Trainer telling my story in hopes that it would change someone's life. I felt like I was making a difference which grew my own Self-Worth.

Armed with Resilience skills and a message, I began a professional speaking career. I was booked to speak at business conferences, resilience conferences, military events, and taught many resilience classes to the military community around the country. In 2016, I wrote a bestselling book called, Decisions: The Power To Overcome Self-Defeating Behaviors. In 2017, I started a live online radio show called, Life Transformation Radio, which I sold in 2021. I was speaking, training, and coaching other Speakers on how to build value in themselves and in their business. I was accepted to speak at my dream event, TEDx, to speak on my topic of, Hacking Your Brain For Success. I felt like I had finally made it. I was going to church. My wife gave birth to two beautiful girls. My military career was intact. Even though in the past I had felt like a failure, I now understood that I truly was made for something great.

Whether I knew it or not, I did become a farmer, of sorts. As I look back on the 30-something years of my life, I had to be abused as a kid. I had to be bullied. I had to join the Military. I had to develop a drinking problem. I had to try and take my life. My mom had to give me that book. I had to talk to Military Chaplains. I had to become a Drill Instructor. I had to become a Master Resilience Trainer. I had to become a Suicide Awareness Trainer. I had to write a book. I had to create a Podcast. I had to have these dark nights of the soul moments. I had to have a story. I had to learn how to tell that story. I had to have a platform to tell my story on, and I had to develop Self-Worth in me before I could develop Self-Worth in others. You cannot give from an empty cup, and you cannot harvest from an empty garden.

Like a farmer tends to his fields, I had to tend to my own gardens. I was not giving a bountiful harvest to those around me. People would pour into me but it would just soak in one ear and out the other. The nutrients didn't land where they needed. The fertilizer of The Word never reached the roots. The care and love only made it to the surface level and my hardened heart would never let my empty cup become filled. The productivity of a farm depends on the health and natural fertility of the soil. If your soil is unhealthy, what nutrients do you need in order to bring it back to life? In farming, you need to study the soil. In life, you need to study yourself and your behavior. In marriage, you need to continue to study your partner. That is how we continue to grow and sustain. As a farmer, he needs to plant seeds. In life, you need to plant seeds in the form of connections made, love given, and gratitude shared. This is how we develop our Self-Worth. We create our Core Values, our seeds. We fill up our cup by living by example, our brand. It is the nutrients to our own soil like watering our garden. We aren't watering our garden with dirty water, so why take in all the negativity of life? We need to water the gardens of our soul with fresh nutrients, like gratitude and positivity. Like a farmer tends his garden to remove weeds, we too must remove the weeds from our own garden. Remove those negative people like weeds from your life. We must be vigilant to find them, be vigilant to prevent their growth, and actively remove them.

Spiritual Resilience is the fertilizer of your life. You don't have to believe in God, that may be my fertilizer, but strengthening your beliefs, principles, and values is how you will prevent that negativity from taking root.

I did become a farmer. Every day, I plant seeds. Every day, I water my life's garden as a spouse, as a father, a Military Serviceman, as a business owner, and as a Christian. Every day, I strive to live by example. No one ever said it would be easy, but the harvest will always be worth it in the end. Find what you were created to be. Find your purpose. You were made for something great!

<u>BIO</u>

Sean Douglas is a U.S. Air Force Veteran, TEDx Speaker, Master Resilience Implementer & Suicide Awareness Trainer, Business Positioning Strategist, International Podcast Host of Create Launch Monetize Podcast, and a Bestselling Author. He's a suicide survivor who hit rock bottom. He believes that you were created for a purpose, and once you unlock your true potential, you will elevate your life, which is why he founded, The Success Corps. Sean works with Entrepreneurs, Speakers, and Business Owners to improve their Positioning in the Market which increases Profitability while decreasing their anxiety and stress so their business thrives.

Website: www.TheSuccessCorps.com
Podcast: https://podcasts.apple.com/us/podcast/create-launch-monetize-podcast/id1542427013

9 7 9 8 5 0 8 2 3 2 6 7 2